A

THREE YEARS' CRUIZE

IN THE

MOZAMBIQUE CHANNEL,

FOR THE

SUPPRESSION OF THE SLAVE TRADE.

BY

LIEUT. BARNARD, R.N.

LONDON:

RICHARD BENTLEY, NEW BURLINGTON STREET,

Publisher in Ordinary to Her Majesty.

1848.

TO

REAR-ADMIRAL THE HON. JOSCELINE PERCY, C.B.

LATE COMMANDER-IN-CHIEF OF THE CAPE OF

GOOD HOPE STATION,

THIS JOURNAL IS DEDICATED

AS A

MARK OF RESPECT.

PREFACE.

THE possibility of effectually suppressing the Slave Trade is a question which is now engaging the serious attention of the Legislature, and has been for some time past the subject of anxious speculation by the Public.

The Author of the following pages has been induced to believe that the revelations contained in them are additions to the knowledge already acquired of this hateful traffic, and accordingly he has published them. He has not deemed it necessary to heighten or to amend the style in which they were originally written, or to withdraw from them their familiar tone. They were addressed to his father, and were intended for the perusal of his relations and friends. The Public, therefore, has a sort of guarantee of the Author's good faith, and will be inclined, he doubts not, to place full reliance on his statements.

LONDON,
MAY, 1848.

CONTENTS.

CHAPTER I.

CHAPTER II.

CONTENTS.

CONTENTS.   xi

CHAPTER V.

Page

Ludicrous Accident. — Azvedo's Hospitality.—Slaves Burnt Alive.—The Black Schooner. — Morgado's Grand Dinner.—Dr. Peters.—The Colonos.—Willing Slaves.—Invitation to a Ball.—A Sail ahead.—Board a Slaver.—Mutiny and Murder.—Mr. Hill's Fifty Days on Board a Slaver.—Wreck of the Julia. The Don Pedro.—The Minerva.—The Pinnace found.—Attempt to heave up the Guns.—Murderer's Reefs.—Anchor in Simon's Bay 134

CHAPTER VI.

Large Export of Slaves.—Natives of the Zoulu Country. —Imminent Danger of a Portuguese Brig.—Hippopotamus Point.—An Old Friend.—Board the Juavo Adelaide.—Interview and Dinner with the Governor of Majunga.—Alexander's Whiskers.—The Governor's Guard.—His Dress.—Punishment of a Culprit. —The Queen of Majunga.—Religion of the Natives. —Suspicious Cruizer.—Horsa Horsa. — Interview with the new Governor of Quillimane.—Capture of a Slave Brig... 163

CHAPTER VII.

Excursion into the Interior.—Establishment of Morgado. —A Dinner with him described.—Resources of the Country.—History of a Slave Brig.—Warned against Lions.—Black Boys Sleeping.—Native Brick-mak-

CHAPTER X.

CHAPTER XI.

A

THREE YEARS' CRUIZE

IN THE

MOZAMBIQUE CHANNEL.

CHAPTER I.

ST. AUGUSTINE'S BAY.—NATIVES OF MADAGASCAR: JIM
BRAVO AND JOHN GREEN.—KING BABA.—TALLEAR
BAY.—NATIVES.—ALGOA BAY.—QUILLIMANE.—HIP-
POPOTAMI.—SENHOR AZVEDO.—CORRUPTION OF POR-
TUGUESE GOVERNORS.—THEIR CONNIVANCE AT THE
SLAVE TRADE.—HOW CARRIED ON.—BANYANS.—
SLAVE CUSTOMS.—NATIVE BLACKSMITHS.—SKILFUL
SWIMMERS.—THIEVES AND EXTORTIONERS.—PASSAGE
OF THE BREAKERS.—GALLANTRY OF MAJOR SMITH.
—PORT NATAL.—BOERS.—CAFFRES.

ON the 9th of December, 1842, we left the
Mauritius for the Mozambique Channel, and
running close round Cape Amber, the north
end of Madagascar, anchored off St. George's
Island on the 21st, and I was sent on shore in
the gig to the town (Mozambique), but finding that the Governor was away, and the

B

season being extremely hot (thermometer
83° on board), we got under weigh the next
morning, so that I shall reserve my description
of the place until a subsequent date, when we
saw more of it.   Our Christmas was spent at
sea, and on the 28th we arrived at St. Augustine's Bay, near the south end of Madagascar.
I had been there before in the Jaseur, in 1830,
and was therefore somewhat prepared to witness the scenes which took place.

As soon as the anchor was let go, the ship
was surrounded by numbers of canoes with
from five to six men or women in each, who,
with their hair tied all over in large knots or
plaited into imitation tails, have a most gro-
tesque appearance to the eye of a stranger.
Some of them are dressed in old shirts or any
articles of wearing apparel they can get from
the ships that call there, but for the most part
they have merely a long cotton cloth wound
round their middle, and they are a fine, strong
and sleek-looking race.   There is a strong
mixture of cunning and ignorance about them,
and their intercourse with Europeans has certainly not improved their morals; and from

the frequent visits of American whalers they
have all acquired sufficient broken English to
carry on a trade, but so interlarded with
swearing and the coarsest language, that one
soon gets disgusted with them.

Our first visitor was Jim Bravo, a tall strong-
looking fellow, about six feet three inches, to
whom the possession of an old uniform cap
imparted an air of authority: he produced
certificates from an American whaler giving him
the character of being more honest than many
of his countrymen, and I have since seen him
on board several merchant-vessels, where, for a
small present, he purchases all kinds of necessaries for them. The next important character
was John Green, or, as they pronounce it,
Dungaree, a noisy rascal, whose ugly and
sinister countenance was only equalled by his
cool impudence;—but his dress must first be
described to enable you to form any adequate
idea of him. A very old duck frock, and unwhisperables of the same material, were be-
spangled all over with the brass scales of an
old chin-stay, American naval buttons, and
dead-eyes of various sorts. Under one of a very

broad pair of dirty cotton braces was an epau-
lette, which, if one might judge from its colour,
had once decked the shoulder of a very old
luff, serving under the star-spangled banner,
and this was kept in countenance by a super-
annuated cap, from under which peered a
restless, roguish-looking eye. In this rig he
bounced on deck, and disdaining even to look
at us poor humble individuals, asked, "Where
the captain?" and thrusting out his dirty paw
to shake him by the hand, commenced an
almost unintelligible harangue, the burden of
which was, "John Green very good man—purser
to Prince Green—Captain very good man—
and suppose he like to make trade, he all the
same—one fadder, one modder, one brodder,
one sister."

After the men's dinner, I went to the Tent
Rock to look for water, but found the
old watercourse dried up, so made sail for
the Dartmouth river, where on landing, we
found Jim Bravo, who conducted us to the
village where Prince Willie (a corruption of
the Prince of Wales) resides, and is the chief
of this part of Madagascar, not owning the

authority of the Queen. We found him holding a palaver with an ambassador and his attendants from King Baba, the chief of a roving and predatory tribe to the northward, about Murderer's Island and its neighbourhood: their object was to form an alliance, and their mode of proceeding was highly picturesque. About a hundred men, each armed with a musket and spear, were seated or rather squatted on their haunches in parties of threes, forming a circle, on one side of which was the old Prince, seated on a mat, blowing a long deliberate cloud, and opposite to him a middle-aged man, seated tailor fashion, and holding forth; and every now and then when he paused, the elders would put in a word edgeways. Our appearance in uniform did not seem to call off the attention of one of them, nor did one of them move, until Jim Bravo spoke to the Prince, who in a polite message to the captain, promised him a visit on the morrow. He is an old man about eighty; a few very long and straggling grey hairs hang about his weatherbeaten countenance, and one of his eyes is in such a dreadful state, that it is quite

horrid to look at it, and reminds one of a
very large bruised bullock's eye covered with
flies, and one is glad to get away from it; so
when he came off on the following day, the
captain made him a present of a cartridge of
powder, and some rum, and sent him on shore
quite pleased.

The next day we made up a party, to go to
Tallear Bay, a place about fifteen miles to the
northward inside the reefs; it consisted of
Molesworth, Alexander, Hill, Denman, and
myself, and we called on our way for the
master of a small Mauritius schooner, from
whom we purchased beads, looking-glasses,
and iron pots, for barter; and, after a tedious
passage, anchored in the Bay about a hundred
yards off shore, and were immediately surrounded by a swarm of canoes, and found it
impossible to keep the natives out of the pinnace; and the head man, called Captain Martin,
young Martin, and young Arabin, seated
themselves in the stern-sheets, and each being
anxious to shew how much more fluent he was
in English than the others, they all spoke together so fast that we were half an hour

making out that they wanted a present before they would barter; so we gave them a looking-glass and a few strings of beads, and Hill, Denman, and myself, landed in a canoe.

A few very small tumble-down huts, cattle-pens in the midst of them, with here and there an old stunted tree on a burning-hot sandy hillock, form their village, and miserable and desolate did it look. After staring about us for a little time, about a dozen fellows with muskets made their appearance, and I must say I looked on them with much distrust; however, I put a good face on the matter, and after they had rigged an awning on the beach, I squatted down in the midst of them. Their great object was to get brandy, which I pretended not to understand; however, I at last said, putting my finger to my nose, "Me understand lee-tle." This made them all laugh heartily and point to me, as much as to say in their own language, "He know plenty too much." So I took advantage of their good humour, and got them to take us off; and not liking their looks, their pressing invitations to remain the night, their decided habits of appropriation and ignorance of the difference of *meum* and *tuum*, and increasing clamour for brandy;—the moment I got into the boat I weighed and made all sail with a fine strong breeze, and nearly towed them all under water before they would let go, without their having obtained anything but a few shells. We might, perhaps, by waiting, have got bullocks, sheep, goats, or our throats cut, as the humour happened to take them. For my part, I would not trust them out of sight of the ship.

We were benighted going down, and got amongst the breakers; so I bore up and anchored off a village about two-thirds of the way down, and would not hear of any one landing; and such a night we had of it! Some of the party wanted to sleep, others would sing, and at last, after spreading the sails for an awning, Hill declared that it was a dreadful alternative, to be either smothered or to sleep in the open air, and rushed out, capsizing all our arrangements, and lying on the top of the covering. I got up to see what was the matter, kicked over the master of the schooner amongst the empty bottles, trod on somebody else's leg, and we all burst into a roar of laughter, which had barely subsided when Hill again shifted his berth, and at last found a soft place among the bottles. We got a few shells in the morning, and .arrived on board about nine A.M.

On January 2nd, 1843, we started for Algoa Bay, where we anchored on the 10th, and I was sent on shore to the town of Port Elizabeth to call on the commandant and magistrate. I found the latter, Captain Lloyd, a most hospitable person, and, hearing that my object was to find a watering-place, he provided a horse for me, and sent his son to show the road; and after riding along the beach for about a mile, we found a small stream; but the landing was so bad, that we determined to water from the town by means of surf boats; and, after remaining here four days, and laying in a good stock of provisions, which are exceedingly good and cheap, left for Quillimane, a Portuguese settlement on the east coast of Africa, in 18° south, and the residence of all the agents for the slave dealers at Rio Janeiro.

On the morning of Sunday, February 5th, 1843, I left for this place in the second cutter, the ship having anchored two days before about eight miles off shore. Alexander and Wrey accompanied me, and not knowing the proper channel or the force of the current, I found myself at daylight considerably to leeward, and after a long pull succeeded in getting through what is called the Boat Channel, where I found the ripple so strong that I was obliged to put the boat, head to sea, and drift in with the flood. I little knew the risk I was running. We found an English schooner, called the Trekboer, from Algoa Bay, at anchor just inside the Point, the captain of which gave us the necessary directions for going up, and some useful hints about getting stock, &c., at the town.

Keeping close along the south shore to avoid the breakers, which extend down the centre of the river nearly to its mouth, we fired away at the numerous wild fowl and curlew: cranes, pelicans, &c., flew screeching over our heads

as if astounded by the unwonted report of a
musket. The banks of the river are so low
that at high water they are flooded, and every
here and there are creeks running up amongst
the mangrove bushes, in which we saw several
large launches which are generally kept in
readiness to embark slaves. The general aspect
of the shore is a succession of sandy patches
and stunted shrubs alternately until about
eight miles from the entrance, where the mangrove bushes grow at the water's edge. In the
back-ground are low spreading green trees,
with here and there a tall cocoa-nut tree
towering above the rest: the shore is strewed
with large trees, torn up by the roots during
the rainy season, when the freshes rush down
with resistless fury.

Every now and then we saw some black
masses, about twenty yards from the shore,
like logs of wood, but on approaching them
found that they were the heads of hippopotami, poking up their noses with a most
unearthly roar; the temptation was great, and
we lowered the sail and pulled in to have a
shot at them: I fancy I struck one in the ear,

or somewhere about the head, for it made a tremendous plunge and dived with a roar. Some distance up the river we observed what we took to be white houses, but found that they were pelicans with their wings spread out to dry. We met and hailed a canoe paddled by six negroes, and as we had just come on the coast it was quite a novelty. At first they did not like to approach us, but a few friendly signs and a little broken Portuguese soon brought them to. They were sitting on the sharp edge of the canoe, a large tree hollowed out, and were all but in a state of nature; we gave them some beads and biscuit and received in return a few bananas.

We had by this time got near the town, which may easily be distinguished from its being in the midst of the only group of cocoa-nut trees near the bend of the river, about fifteen miles from its mouth; and just as we had got ready to land, down came one of those unexpected tropical showers out of a passing cloud, which wet you through whilst you are wondering where it comes from. On landing, we were carried up a muddy beach by blacks; and the one who made an attempt to take me soon found that I was no feather weight and called another to his assistance. We rewarded them with a few beads, and went to the house of the pilot and port-captain, whom we found in his porch smoking with a friend: he treated us with great civility and *aqua ardiente*, and directed us to Senhor Azvedo, the first appearance of whose domicile led us to expect something very superior, and we were not disappointed, for after we had waited a short time, examining numerous pictures with which the room was hung, in came a middle-aged man with a most gentlemanly air, and welcomed us in a very cordial manner, and, after offering us a glass of good sherry, accompanied us to the Governor's, as I expressed a wish to pay my respects.

We were received at the entrance of his residence by the captain of a Portuguese brig-of-war at anchor off the town. I found he was a Frenchman, named Trou; but I shall have to speak of him hereafter. The Governor made his appearance apparently from dinner,

and after the usual compliments on these
occasions, and lots of bows and grimaces, we
made our exits. His name was Don Carlos
Fernando da Costa, about forty-five years of
age, and a commander in the Portuguese navy.
The tide and wind being against us, I yielded
to the solicitations of our host. to remain
the night: he made us as much at home as
possible, and I had a most interesting conversation with him, which proved the commencement of much important and useful information; and though my ideas on many of the
subjects I am about to relate are now much
altered, I shall transcribe them from the notes
I took at the time, when fresh from England,
and greatly struck with the novelty of every
thing round me.

It appears that the Governors come out
here with the avowed purpose of making a
fortune by conniving at the slave trade and
other peculations, their salary being only 1,000
dollars per annum, paid in blue Dungaree.
Consequently, the good of the colony is very
far from their thoughts, and when Don Carlos
arrived, he found Azvedo collector of the cus-

toms, whose duty it was, after the abolition of the slave trade, to seize any vessels, or their cargoes, engaged in that traffic. About that time information was received of a brig's being in the offing ready to take in a cargo of slaves from Point Tangalane, on which Azvedo demanded twenty soldiers from the Governor, who paid no attention to the request for twenty-four hours; consequently the traces only were found of the blacks having been removed, which was effected most probably by the connivance of the Governor, who is said to receive 7,000 dollars from each slaver, which he shares with the captain of the brig.

From this time an ill-feeling arose between the Governor and collector, which was soon turned into rancour by the following circumstance. The master of the Trekboer having landed three cheeses, with an order from Azvedo, they were seized by the soldiers and sold by auction; and it may be easily conceived how bitter they were against each other when, in endeavouring to outbid, one cheese sold for eighteen dollars, and the others for sixteen and thirteen, and were broken up and given to the dogs. Thence ensued a paper war, which ended in the dismissal of. Azvedo, who professed himself extremely anxious to give every information tending to the capture of slavers; and he assured me that if we remained off Quillimane for twenty-one days, our time would not be lost, as four or five vessels were expected from Rio, and that one ship had already been off and made her signal. In corroboration of this there was a great collection of slaves in chains in the town, and Flavell, our coxswain, who spoke a little Portuguese, learnt that they were expecting a vessel daily.

The slavers do not generally enter the river, but make a private signal, which their agents answer on shore, and the slaves are sent out in the launches we observed in the creeks. I heard that from twelve to fourteen had gone off to Rio in the previous six months, but I much doubt there having been so many.

About six o'clock we sat down to a sumptuous dinner, well served and capitally cooked; not a bad thing after a hard day's cruise. The attendance was good and highly picturesque, the blacks standing behind each chair like ebony statues, their arms folded and their eyes fixed on their temporary master's plate, which disappeared in a twinkling when empty. Mangoes, pine-apples, bananas, cocoa-nut in the shape of an excellent sweet-meat, and preserves, formed the dessert; and after our worthy host had proposed the healths of Captain Wyvill and absent friends, we quitted the table, and the boat's crew took our places, and got such a blow-out as they didn't expect, and were most probably the first of their families who had ever used silver-handled knives and forks.

The men slept in the boat, and we remained on shore; but the oppressive heat, musquitoes, over-fatigue, and anxiety, banished sleep from my eyes, although Alexander and Wrey snored away all night. In addition, there was one continued roar and flash of thunder and lightning, which ended about six in the morning with torrents of rain and an awful thundersquall.

I was greatly puzzled how to return all the hospitality and handsome conduct of our host, who would not allow me to pay for any

thing. All was *un petit cadeau*, and he loaded
us with bananas, pine-apples, mangoes, &c.; and
on an old fellow's trying to impose on us, he
kicked him out of the house, and had all the
ducks and chickens in his own yard caught and
put into the boat, accompanying us to the
beach, and waving his hand as long as we
were in sight.

Whilst at his house we had a visit from
upwards of a dozen Banyans, who came to
find out if there was any news, or in other
words, if any prizes had been taken: their
vessel had been taken by the Curlew, and condemned for having a quantity of rice not in
their manifest. They dress in the Arab style,
and are the Jews of this country: their history
I will give in a future page.

There were not more than twenty-four Europeans in the town, and the number of troops
for the districts of Quillimane, Senna, and Tete,
were 340, consisting of convicts, mulattos, and
blacks, miserably clad and worse fed. The
blacks were computed at 3,000,000.

On arriving on board on Monday, February
the 6th, and giving the above information, the

captain determined to cruise in the neighbourhood for some time; and on the 16th I was
again sent up to the town in the barge, taking
the dingy with me, and accompanied by the
Rev. P. G. Hill and Denman. We had a
famous run up of two hours and a half, and
were received by Senhor Azvedo in the same
friendly manner, and remained on shore during
the next day, which gave us an opportunity
of exploring. Every thing appeared to denote
the unavoidable existence of fever and disease:
the swampy rice-grounds surround the town for
miles and miles, with creeks running through
them full of mud and slime, exposed at low
water to the rays of a scorching tropical sun.
Having been ordered not to sleep on shore, I
covered in the boat well with the sails; but
the dew was so heavy that two parts of new
canvas were wet through and all but dripping;
and in the morning, after a broken night's
rest, we got on shore and took a good stretch
out amongst high rank grass and anything but
terra firma, the musquitoes swarming in such
myriads that we were literally covered and
driven half crazy. We laid in a good stock of

fowls, pigs, fruit, &c. Our worthy host still refusing payment we sent him a handsome present from the anchorage.

Some of the customs of the slaves are interesting, amongst others that of wearing bangles or solid brass rings, reaching from the ancle to the knee, gradually increasing in size: they are a great mark of distinction amongst them, and are worn by the women in charge of the white children, and the girls who act as ladies' maids. Nothing can degrade them more than depriving them of these ornaments, and a woman who would not wince at the lash would weep bitterly if her bangles were taken from her, notwithstanding they are so heavy that they often lacerate the foot, and make them look most awkward when walking. Their mode of salutation is curious: they first stand quite upright with their heels together, and then make an inclination by bending the knees and clapping their hands twice.

Amongst the slave population the women work as hard as the men, and are punished in the same brutal manner. I saw several women, all but in a state of nudity, strung together

with heavy chains supported by an iron ring
round the throat, and digging up the ground
with hoes.   This I was told was for stealing
rice; but whatever the crime, it was a most
horrid and degrading sight to an Englishman.
Some of the men are very intelligent and work
in gold, silver, and iron, with tools and appara-
tus of the most primitive description: the bel-
lows are made of deer-skins with two pieces of
bamboo at the mouth, which is opened and
closed with the finger and thumb as it is moved
up or pressed down, one being in each hand, and
the nozles being introduced into a piece of
brick-work on the ground communicating by two
holes with a charcoal fire.   The blacksmith sits
on his haunches, and for an anvil generally has
a-pig of ballast: with these rough implements
they make even pintles and gudgeons for large
vessels, hinges for doors, slave shackles, and
chains.   The workers in gold use a blow-
pipe, and draw the wire through a bit of lead
bored with holes gradually diminishing in size,
and I have seen some very handsome ornaments made by them.

In working down the river with a foul wind

we saw, for the first time, a huge hippopotamus quite out of the water running at a smart
trot along a sand-bank. Hill fired at him,
and he immediately plunged into the water
and appeared inclined to become better acquainted with us; but having heard stories of
their biting pieces out of boats, we got put of
the way as quickly as possible, but soon after
grounded on a sand-bank and remained there
a whole tide; and after a fruitless attempt to
get out against the flood we had to anchor until
the ebb made, when I stood out and burnt a
bluelight. The night being pitch dark, and the
ship answering it, I got on board at nine
o'clock, but excepting in a case of great neces-
sity I would never run so great a risk again.
At that time, however, I had no dearbought
experience.

On the 21st, we found twenty-five tons of
water brackish, and stood across to St. Augustine's Bay, and I was sent on shore to superintend the watering party. Pitching a tent under
a tamarind-tree on a patch of sand between
two branches of the river and about three-
quarters of a mile from the Bay, and to facili-

tate the ascent of the boats against the
freshes, hawsers were laid down for upwards of
half a mile with a nun buoy at the end. I
had scarcely got my tent all right, when canoes
came from all directions to barter sheep, kids,
fowls, and vegetables for beads, looking-glasses,
and powder, and I soon found that I had a
knowing and grasping set to deal with. The
next morning I found some of my new friends
waiting for me with milk, which they presented
very civilly, and I as gratefully received; but
they were not long in showing me that "nothing for nothing" was their creed, and I was
literally thronged by as importunate and per-
severing beggars as can be well imagined. Their
cry was "Give beady to piccineene, Leetenant,
you good friendy to me. I give you millik and
ebery ting: oh Leetenant, you bigger man, all
the same as Captain, spose you give me
clouty; you my fadder, my modder, my brodder,
my sister." All this was amusing enough for a
short time, and I made them dance and sing,
bought their mats and spears and fed them
with biscuit, but I invariably found that they
were dissatisfied at not getting more, and at
last they became very tiresome.

On the third day I witnessed certainly a most novel sight, viz., a whole village of men, women, and children, swimming across a branch of the river. With one hand they held their clothes above their heads, and sometimes a young infant, and on arriving on the opposite side deposited them on the bank and swam about like water-dogs, making a very loud noise in concert with the hollow of their hands. Soon after they all came on shore, completing their toilet in about a second, and their skins being well oiled, they made their appearance in the tent as dry as possible. Several of the women were very good-looking, and soon got on very free and easy terms with me, for if I laid down to take a nap, I was sure to find, when I awoke, that two or three of them had made a pillow of me, which with their greasy and populous heads was anything but agreeable; and I made all the rest dreadfully jealous and clamorous by rigging up the head of a young girl with narrow white tape, a pair of earrings, and a necklace of beads, which with a fathom of clouty set her off to great advantage. I christened her " Friendly," and she used always afterwards to bring me milk.

The day before our departure from St
Augustine's Bay, they showed their pilfering
propensities by taking the copper forelocks of
the gun-carriages and screws of the tangent-
sights, and in the end walked off with the nun
buoy which we had used for watering. Alexander and I tried very hard to bargain for
some bullocks, but they wanted ten dollars for
them, which we considered an exorbitant price,
and offered eight, but they wouldn't come to
terms, and as they began to collect in large
numbers, well armed, and to cast a very wistful
eye on the dollar bag, I parted company with
them as fast as possible. The shells here are
numerous but not rare, and they barter them
for empty bottles, beads, and anchor buttons,
and they are so cunning that they never show
all the good ones at once, but produce them
one by one from the folds of their clouty. I
learnt their numbers as far as ten; they are as
follows:—

1	2	3	4	5	6	7	8	9	10
Esaw	Rona	Tela	Effa	Lima	Enna	Feeta	Vasla	Theva	Foula

We left them on March 4th, and crossed to
Natal, where we arrived on the 12th.

C

Port Natal is in latitude 29° 53′, S., and longitude 30° 57′, E.; the anchorage is about a mile from the shore, in ten fathoms, and extremely dangerous, being quite open to the southeast, and the entrance over the bar is not safe above twelve times in a month, and cannot at any time be depended on for two hours. The day we arrived I was sent on shore in the cutter with the purser, a heavy ground swell setting in from seaward directly on the bar, and had I not observed a boat belonging to the Fawn, inside the breakers, looking out for us, I should not have attempted the passage. As it was, I made a dash for it, but the boat's crew being unaccustomed to a surf, were taken by surprise, and could not attend to my orders. We consequently broached-to, lost two oars, and nearly tore off the gunnel: we observed a large shark following us the whole way, and I was joking the purser, telling him that it was looking out for him, little thinking how soon one of us might have made a meal for him.

On landing, we were received by Lieut. Nourse, of the Fawn, Capt. Durnford, com-

manding the Point, and several officers from the
Camp, all quite delighted at seeing a new face
or two, and as the boat was to remain all night,
a ride to the Camp was proposed, and after
being pent up in a ship so long, a good gallop
was delightful. The road had been cut through
the woods, and we soon arrived at the spot which
will be ever memorable for the gallant defence
of Captain, now Major Smith, and about fifty
men, who intrenched themselves behind wagons,
and held out for twenty-six days against 2,400
Boers, well armed, and assisted by three pieces
of artillery in commanding positions. Against
this overwhelming force they protected themselves by heaping sand between the wheels of
their wagons, which enclosed their tents ;
these were perfectly riddled, and their owners
saw their little all destroyed from the
trenches ; and at last, after having been three
days on a reduced allowance of horse-flesh,
they were relieved by the Southampton,
whose shells soon drove the enemy from the
Point.

When we were there, the force was 312 men
and officers: 100 remain at the Point, the rest

at the Camp, which is about one and a-half
mile distant, and has now assumed the appearance of a regular fortification, built with
turf, and loopholed, with here and there a
battery of field-pieces and howitzers.   Major
Smith received us kindly, and gave us some
idea of the Boers, who seem to be a most
ignorant race of men, and are in daily expectation of receiving assistance from Holland.
They believe that the story of a war with
China, has been got up by the English to in-
timidate them, and make themselves appear a
great nation.

After being most hospitably entertained at
the messes, we, the next day, sent off bullocks
and all kinds of stores for a long cruise.   The
Caffres come in daily and hold a market,
bringing pumpkins, vegetables, poultry, and
native curiosities, which they barter for mere
trifles, their wants being but few, and a few
strips of tiger-skin furnishing them with a full
dress.

The bar of Natal is extremely dangerous
and treacherous, frequently becoming furious
quite unexpectedly, a large wall of surf rearing

its crest, and towering above the boat without the least warning, and now that the Fawn is paid off, whose officers were always on the *qui vive* in case of accidents, the danger of crossing will be increased tenfold.

CHAPTER II.

On the 23rd of March, 1843, I made my
third trip to Quillimane with the purser, and
finding that our friend Azvedo was from home,
we were rather puzzled what to do ; but I went
to look for our old friend the pilot, whom we
found smoking in the porch of Senhor Morgado's, who kindly invited us to dinner, and
shortly after we had sat down I was agreeably
surprised by the appearance of Senhor Azvedo,
who had heard of our arrival, and came immediately to see us. In the evening we had a
long conversation, and I learnt that during
our absence the Lily had taken two Brazilian

barques, and driven a schooner on shore, and
that there were two others expected in the
course of three weeks, one empty, and the
other with a full cargo; and the people of
Quillimane were so incensed against Azvedo,
whom they suspected of giving me information,
that he was obliged to keep an armed force in
his house every night.

In the evening we adjourned to our old quarters, and were highly interested and amused with
a native dance, the principal performers being
three kings who had come from the interior to
trade. Their sable majesties were distinguished
from their followers by a great number of bangles made from the hippopotamus' hide, reaching
from the wrist to six inches above the elbow, and
they each drank a tumbler of *aqua ardiente*,
as if it had been water. The dance commenced
with sundry uncouth gestures, and twisting of
body and limbs in slow time, gradually increasing in energy until the excitement was at the
highest pitch; and they at last took a round
turn and fell back exhausted amongst the surrounding crowd, who kept constantly clapping
their hands, and joined in a monotonous chorus,

their bodies bent forward and eyes glistening
with delight, giving every now and then a
scream of encouragement to the dancer.

In the course of the evening, the masters of
two American brigs came in, and I found that
their names were the Anna and Kentucky:
they were loading with mud for ballast, and
they were anxious that I should look at them;
however, I learnt quite sufficient to feel certain
that, had not the coast been well guarded,
they would have delivered one of them over
for slaves—in fact, the master of the Anna
told me that propositions had been made to
him.

I slept on board the Anna that night,
mooring my boat astern, and little thought
that I should ever command her as a prize.
In the morning I had, whilst at Azvedo's, a
visit from one of the kings, to whom I presented one of the buttons of my jacket, which
has now the honour of being hung to one of
his majesty's ear-rings.

We had a specimen of the barbarous music
of the country from a travelling blind man,
who had his eyes put out in his own country

for winking them at one of his king's wives, and afterwards fled to the Portuguese possessions, where he lives by going from door to door with a companion, who commences by shaking a calabash full of pease in measured time. This was taken up by the blind man, whose voice gradually rose to a tremendous pitch, when he appeared much excited, and applying a ram's, or rather a mero's horn, with a square hole in it, to his mouth, produced the most unearthly sound I ever heard. The burden of the song seemed to be, "Hoy yoy hoy;" a blow of the horn, "Goulah." He was clothed with the skin of some animal, and, with his sightless sockets, looked a most miserable object.

I found three of my boat's crew had gone off during the night, taking a musket and ammunition with them. I immediately applied to Azvedo, who sent twenty of his blacks in chase, and I followed in a machila— a cot slung under a large bamboo covered with zebra skins, and carried by four men—who rattled me along at a smart trot, and seemed highly amused at my fancying they were tired after carrying me two miles and offering to get out to walk. My three men were found under a tree about four miles from Quillimane; and a mercy indeed it was that they escaped with their lives, as, the very night before, a negro, a negress, and a dog, were carried off by the tigers, not very far from the spot where it appears they had slept.

I left on the 25th, but did not reach the ship for twenty-six hours, the current running so strong to the northward that I was obliged to anchor, and wait for the ship to drop down to me. Between this and the 31st it blew a gale, and the boats were not able to leave; but on that day I was ordered to take the barge and pinnace up for wood, and, when on the point of shoving off, a sail was observed in the offing, and I was directed to cut her off if possible. In about an hour I caught sight of her top-gallant sail, and with oars and sails chased her for six hours, beating a whale-boat belonging to the Portuguese brig in fine style, when night hid her from our sight, and I stood back in quest of the pinnace; but not finding her, I bore up for the ship, then under all sail in chase. When within half a mile of her, I shewed a light, and observed the ship immediately heave in stays, and I fancied I was seen, until I found her bearing down upon me; and before anything could be done, our sails were becalmed, and the boat was under the bows.

Providentially, they had thrown all aback, and deadened the ship's way. Still I had ordered every man to look out for a rope, and get on board in the event of the boat's filling, and I found myself with Hill very affectionately embracing the figure-head; but he never then, or ever afterwards, hinted that he thought my conduct incautious or at all blameable, until I saw my character reflected on in the pamphlet entitled, "Fifty Days on board a Slaver." Much he knew about it! Fortunately, the boat escaped with the loss of her mainyard; and after ascertaining the bearing of the river, which was west by north twenty miles, I started afresh, and in four hours anchored in two and a half fathoms close to the shore, and in the morning was much relieved at seeing the pinnace not far from me.

We soon worked up to the bar, and got

on board H.M.F.M. brig, Gentil Liberador, commanded by Trou, a Frenchman, who gave us a good breakfast, and fished my main-yard, when I proceeded to Quillimane, and loaded with wood ready to start the next morning, which I did about seven A.M., and found all the requisites for a good breakfast in the boat, sent by Azvedo.

We had some difficulty in crossing the bar, but reached the ship at two P.M., when I was ordered to prepare to take charge of the barge and cutter, with a fortnight's provisions, to cruise off the river, whilst the ship went to the northward in search of the brigantine we had chased. At sunset I left the ship, Mr. Thomas (mid.) having charge of the cutter, and anchored about 10 P.M. outside the bar, and spread the rain awnings.

I observed a sail at daylight, and after making sail in chase, and preparing the arms, found it to be my old friend Trou in the Gentil coming out of the river. The next day I paid him a visit, and found that he had written a note inviting me and my officers to dine with him, as it was the Queen of Portugal's birthday. He received us on deck, and had a very nice cool place rigged up with national flags; and of course we were bound to show how much we felt his hospitality; and after drinking sundry complimentary toasts, we ended, as is the Portuguese custom, by drinking the Queen's health. The next day I examined his charts with him, and gained all the information I could respecting the slave trade.

It appears, that any number of slaves may be obtained and shipped from Quillimane itself at a few hours' notice, and that the Governors have been in the habit of receiving fixed bribes from the slave dealers, whose launches are always ready to start the moment a ship makes her private signal. There are baracoons at the different rivers to the northward and southward of Quillimane, from Quizungo, inside Fogo Island, down to Luabo, the last of the mouths of the Zambesi: the Banyans are also carrying on the traffic from point to point. I continued outside the bar cruising with the brig, generally standing off about thirty miles and returning in the evening, for I found the weather so fine that I was glad to escape the miasma and musquitoes which abound in the river.

On the 9th, I stood out and returned with the brig as usual, but missed her after she had anchored; and the current was running so strong that the boat could not pull up, so I had to anchor in shore considerably to leeward of the flag-staff, and from this time our troubles commenced. In the morning at daylight I stood to sea ready for the sea breeze, and when I fancied myself well to windward, tacked and stood in shore, and found that a day's work put me twenty miles to windward, so that, when I made the land, I ran for a point very much like the one at the entrance of the river, and did not find out my mistake until upwards of twenty miles to leeward, with only one breaker of water and a prospect of being three or four days getting back against the current which had already drifted us so far in a short time. All that night I was on the alert, taking advantage of every little flaw of wind off the land, and pulling occasionally; by this means I gained about eight miles, and at daylight could just see

the point I so much wished to gain; but the
wind came strong against me, and I did not
make a mile in four hours; and the weather
looking threatening, I anchored and spread the
sails to catch rain, but got very little. However
it brought a fair wind with it, and at night we
found ourselves in smooth water off the flag-
staff, and anchored in six fathoms; served out
a reduced allowance of grog with the last of
our water, and made all snug for a quiet night;
but after being asleep about an hour, I was
roused by the disagreeable intelligence that the
cutter astern of me had been nearly swamped,
and that we had drifted into two and a-half
fathoms amongst the breakers.

The danger was most imminent, and we
lost no time in getting the boat's head to
sea under the oars, which the men fagged at
incessantly for five hours, not making an inch
head-way. All this time the rain was lashing
down in torrents, blinding everybody and rendering it quite impossible to give the necessary orders to keep the boat's end on;
consequently we shipped some very heavy
seas, and Thomas and myself had quite as

much as we could manage to keep the water under with two large buckets. Fortunately, the current drifted us a little off as well as along the land, and we anchored on the edge of the breakers until a breeze sprang up and enabled us to put to sea, thankful for our narrow escape. Luckily, our clothes had been kept dry under the tarpaulings, and I made all hands shift and gave them some spirits, and just as I was standing into the river I saw the ship, and right glad was I to get on board.

I found that the ship had taken the brigantine : she was called the Progresso, and had four hundred and fifty slaves on board, shipped at Quizungo, after we had chased her. She gave them a seven hours' run and did not heave to until the musketry reached her sails. This good news was counterbalanced by the death of our poor old purser, Mitchell, who had his nervous system so worked upon by the accident at Natal, and our subsequent cruises, that he fretted himself to death without any apparent bodily disease ; for he came down in the gun-room, put his head between his hands, and made up his mind to die. The Captain took him into his cabin, and every thing was done for him, but he refused all consolation, and got out of his cot by himself the very day he died. Shortly after his death a small white bird was seen perched on the cot just over the head of the body, which gave rise to numerous speculations among the superstitious.

A day or two afterwards we fell in with the Progresso, and I accompanied Dr. Kittle on board to pick out fifty of the most healthy boys to take to the ship, that the others might have more room, and the scene on board beggars all description. On the day she was captured the slaves broke adrift, broke open the casks of *aqua ardiente*, which some of them drank in large quantities: others took salt water, salt beef, and pork, and raw fowls, in consequence of which fifty died the first night, which unfortunately was squally; and to save the vessel the poor wretches were obliged to be kept below, or run the risk of being washed overboard. Previous to this, however, many of the dead bodies were seen on the slave-deck by our men who went down for water, and others were in such a state from their excesses, that in all probability the mortality would have been nearly as great, even had they not been kept below.

We saw several poor sickly skeletons lying on the deck, evidently dying and much disfigured by having been trodden on or crushed underneath the others: they could just gasp, and now and then open their lips whilst an orange was squeezed on them. The others were all covered with craw-craws and itch, and were scratching large sores all over them and howling like maniacs for water. I went on the slave-deck, and half the blacks were then on it, who gave their sign of welcome by clapping their hands in concert. Poor Alexander, who had charge of her, looked dreadfully fagged, and calling me on one side asked me to speak to Mr. Hill, who had been allowed by the Captain to take a passage in her, and beg him not to interfere with the duty of the vessel as he had done, for the men were getting dissatisfied at being spoken to by a civilian; and if he persisted in going on in the same way, it would be necessary to make a report of it to Captain Wyvill and have him

removed. I accordingly pointed out to him
in the strongest manner I could, how much
he would add to Alexander's anxiety, and
what unpleasant feelings he would give rise
to, if he in any way interfered with his
orders.

After this, I was on board once or twice,
and everything appeared to go on more
smoothly; but subsequent events, and the
appearance of "Fifty Days on board a
Slaver," showed how unfortunate it was that
a man should have been allowed to remain
to produce a statement, which, though true
as far as it went, left much to be understood
or imagined, and which tended to throw a
slur on the character of an active and deserv-
ing officer, who nearly fell a victim to his
anxiety and exertions.

The slave-deck measured forty-six feet long,
twenty-five feet wide, and three feet, six inches
high. Of the fifty that we took on board, forty-
nine arrived safely at the Cape, one having
fallen into a tub during the night, and being
too weak to crawl out, was smothered. We
managed to clothe them all, cutting up table-

covers, old green baize, and each contributing
something. They were numbered and divided
into two gangs, and a captain chosen from
among them for each gang. They were made
to run round the decks, for they were so
pinched with the cold, that had it not been
for exercise they would have doubled up like
bootjacks and died.

On our way to the Cape we touched at
Algoa Bay, and arrived at Simon's Bay, on
May 5th; and although we did not sail until
the 26th, the prize had not then arrived, and
we were in a great state of anxiety about her
for many months. On our way back to our
cruising ground, we called at Natal with the
Hon. Henry Cloete, Commissioner, and took
in bullocks, &c.; but the bar became suddenly
so rough that the galley was detained inside
three days, and was then got off with much
difficulty.

On June 15th, 1843, we anchored off Quillimane in company with H. M. brig, Lily, and
I was sent to the town in the pinnace, Molesworth accompanying me. We were received on
landing by my old friend Azvedo, who seemed

quite delighted to see us, and told me that soon after our departure, the place had become very sickly and a very large proportion of the inhabitants had died.

On waiting on the Governor, I found that he was convalescent, although he still looked very ill. I had to offer some explanation respecting an affair which the Lily had had with the Portuguese brig of war. It appears that the former drove a brigantine on shore, but a fast pulling whale-boat of the latter boarded her afterwards and took possession before the Lily's boats, which were sent the next day and which set fire to the vessel, and took out her mainmast. This was construed into invading the Portuguese territory, and was a fine opportunity to talk of wounded honour, &c. However, he gradually sobered down, and at last declared that he should be glad to abide by the admiral's decision; and all our fine speeches being exhausted, I was glad to escape to my old quarters, having a splitting headache from exposure to the sun all day.

Azvedo seemed much gratified at some-presents which I presented to him from the captain and officers; amongst others was an immense round of fresh beef, which, for convalescents, they managed to convert into vanishing fractions in an astonishingly short time. Two of the guests were recognized by Molesworth as having been in his charge as prisoners on board the receiving ship at Rio; and one of them told us that he had made nine clear voyages with slaves, and been taken the tenth. His name is Velozo, and he was married a week after this to a chamois-leather-coloured lady, with an immense property in slaves and the best house at Quillimane, where I have since met with great hospitality and kindness.

On strolling out in the morning, our eyes met certainly a most *un*-English sight. From two to three hundred negresses with hoes were making a wide road from a large house to the church for the funeral procession of the mother of Senhor Isidore, the collector of customs, who had died in the night, and whose slaves they were. At four in the afternoon all the gentlemen in the place assembled at Azvedo's, dressed in black, and went in a body to the house of the deceased. We took up our station opposite the entrance of the church, and had a famous view of the whole affair. First came a sturdy black, bearing a large blue cornet with a white cross on a very long pole; it was kept horizontal by two blacks, who held each a brace, another going before ringing a bell: next came a silver crucifix, then followed the priest and his attendants, chanting a monotonous-sounding death-song immediately before the coffin, which was followed by the mourners, the Governor in full uniform and his secretary being the chief. On entering the church, the body was placed on a raised platform surrounded by tall candles and large pans of incense, and to each of the procession was given about a yard and a-half of wax candle. The priest then commenced to chant the funeral service in unintelligible Latin, and at last made such a horrid squalling, that some of the principal performers laughed outright. With the exception of this, the whole thing was decently conducted, and the service being

ended, the troops were drawn up, and fired
three volleys. This is the first and only
time I ever heard of a woman being buried
with military honours. The following day we
returned to the ship, blazing away at numbers
of hippopotami on the way down; but their
skin is impenetrable to lead, and the blacks
kill them with about an inch of iron bar.

On the 26th of June I boarded the United
States' brig Chipoli, bought at Rio, and sent
with the officers and part of the crew of the
United States' corvette Concorde, which had
been wrecked on the bar of the River Macuzé,
twenty-three miles to the northward of Quillimane, to recover and dispose of her stores.
On the 30th, thinking that the brig might
bring some news from Rio, I was sent up in the
barge, taking with me Baron Lehenson, Jago,
and Bagley (midshipmen) to shew them the
town. I went on board the brig on my way
up, and was agreeably surprised at finding
Azvedo on board, who, with Dr. Tuckerman,
took a passage in the barge after we had
received much civility from the American
officers, who insisted on our taking a glass of
champagne with them.

The following day I was requested to act as interpreter between the Governor and Lieutenant Gardner, commanding the Chipoli, who had been sent by the American commodore at Rio to recover what he could of the Concorde's stores, all idea of recovering the ship having been given up. An account of her loss may not be uninteresting. Her Captain had received information that there were two American brigs at Quillimane engaged in the slave trade, and having no chart of the coast, was running it down with a fine fair wind and smooth water. As he approached the land, the water became discoloured, and the officer of the watch sent several messages to the captain, saying that he considered the ship was running into danger. He was, however, disregarded, and not even a leadsman was ordered into the chains, and the captain had just mounted the poop, and desired them to try for soundings, when she struck. Unfortunately it was the top of high water, and the moment the ebb made, a tremendous sea got up, and she bumped so heavily, that her guns were obliged to be thrown overboard.

D

For four days she tried her strength to the
utmost, and her solid fitted-in timbers alone
saved her, the tide leaving her in two feet at
low water. At last they managed to force her
over the bar under the foresail, with the loss
of seventeen feet of her main-keel, and nearly
the whole of her planking on her bottom: they
then sent the boats up the river, thinking it
was the Quillimane, and after ascending fifty
miles, walked across the country to the town,
from whence assistance was sent; and the captain and purser went round in the gig, and
returning again against the advice of Azvedo,
a pilot, they were drowned on crossing the
bar; the black cook dived three times for the
captain, and got on shore after swimming
seven hours.

I learnt that we might daily expect a vessel
intended for the slave trade, purchased from
the Americans at Rio, and fitted ostensibly
as a whaler, but capable of carrying 800
blacks. Numbers of slaves are being constantly brought from the interior and kept
in the neighbourhood of Quillimane ready for
embarkation, and are considered as much an

article of trade, as ivory and gold-dust, but they seldom sell the domestic, or slaves born at the place, except for punishment; and a threat to send them to the "Negriers," is frequently more effective than a flogging.

On our arrival off the coast, the price of a slave fell from 30 to 10 dollars, and the capture of three vessels, and wreck of another, had frightened them not a little. American vessels are generally purchased at Rio by Brazilians, and bring out a cargo under their original colours, and at the last moment change crews, take in fittings from Quillimane, and run a cargo of slaves; and from what I have heard, I feel certain that one of the American brigs which I saw so much of at the town, was prevented from doing so by our being in the neighbourhood.

Hitherto the Governors of Quillimane, and all the Portuguese possessions on this coast, have had merely nominal pay, but have invariably made large fortunes in a very few years by conniving at the slave trade, a stipulated sum being paid for each black; and I am told that the late Governor made 15,000 dollars in three months. At present the Governor-General at Mozambique, General R. L. D'Abreu de Lima, who served during the whole of the Peninsular war, and was educated in Ireland, has determined to do his best to put down the trade, and in August commences a round of visits to his different dependencies to put things in order. Much might be done by preventing a larger collection of slaves than are requisite for domestic purposes, whereas at present any number may be shipped at a few hours' notice; but whilst the Governors are so badly paid and are old officers sent by the Ministers for the express purpose of amassing riches in these pest-holes, it cannot be expected that they will refuse the customary fees merely to be laughed at in their own country, or praised up as fine honourable fellows by a small party in England, and most probably be poisoned by their next door neighbour.

The masters are absolute and can award severe punishment without trial, and every here and there slaves may be seen chained together by sixes and sevens, working in the fields for theft. Their pilfering propensities are incurable, and I saw a glaring instance of it in one of Azvedo's boys who waited on us whilst up there. He had, whilst we turned our backs, whipped several cigars out of an open box and concealed them about his person; three blacks were summoned on the spot, and he was led away to work in chains for fifteen days; but flogging seems to be seldom resorted to.

In the evening I stood interpreter between the Governor and American officers, and afterwards slept in the boat, finding our new rain-awnings of the greatest service, as the dew was very heavy; and in the morning we could not see one end of the boat from the other. However we landed, and took a walk, much to the astonishment of the inhabitants who never think of shewing their noses until nine o'clock, but even with all this care, the climate and fever have left them mere wrecks of themselves, and I have frequently been addressed by a poor wan-looking creature who a few months before was a strong hale man, and not one of them is free from the liver or spleen. Still an occasional visit without exposure at night is not attended with any bad effects; but if any of the boats' crews remain all night on shore, they generally have a touch of the fever.

I took on board with me a fine intelligent black boy, whose freedom Azvedo offered me if I would take care of him, and as he had always attended us I was glad to snatch him from his degraded country. His name is Jose Tembah, and I was fortunate in getting him a kind and good mistress at the Cape, where he is now, two years after the above, doing well. He is an excellent servant, and is being educated. He sometimes threatens to return to the "Capitaine," as he calls me, but does not mean it, and is as happy as possible.

The morning of July 10th, 1843, which had been settled as the day on which I was to take the boats up the river for water, was anything but promising, a fresh breeze blowing from south-east, and a heavy swell setting on the bar; and I ought to have been warned of the great risk I was about to run, but at that time I had passed so often without any accident, that I had become foolhardy, and very dearly bought the experience which has since made me much more prudent.

The captain had exchanged the jolly-boat for a gig, sharp at both ends, but with much less beam than a whale-boat; we had raised her one streak, and being anxious to try her, I took the lead on shoving off, having with me ·Denman and Law, six men, and several bags; but finding her too deep, I advised Denman and Law to get into the pinnace or barge, and put also two heavy bags into the latter; when close to the bar I hove to, to bale out dry, and practise the men for crossing a surf. On entering the breakers, I found them much heavier than I had anticipated, and from the first, saw that it would be quite a mercy if we crossed safely. However, we got over four breakers beautifully, the boiling foam taking us with it at a most awful rate; the fifth followed us like an overhanging mountain, with its crest in the act of curling, and we rose to it just as it broke, becoming, as it were, a component part of the foam. My feeling was that of intense anxiety, and I at one time thought it would pass us, and had an en-

couraging "all right" on the top of my tongue,
when the angry surf boiled up afresh. There
was a crash, a cry, and in an instant we were
struggling in the breakers, and never were men
rescued from a more hopeless situation. My
first impulse was to dive from under the boat,
and just as I rose to the surface I found myself grappled by a man who could not swim,·
whom I endeavoured to shake off, but finding
that I could keep him up, told him to keep his
hand on my shoulder, and took him to the
boat, which kept constantly turning round and
round like a cask; and the seas constantly
breaking over us gave us so little breathing
time that nearly all hope of being saved was
taken away. It was a most awful moment, and
all the people, places, and things I had ever
seen, seemed concentrated and present at the
same instant to my mind's eye with a startling
distinctness; then the misery of being cut off
from all, in rude health, unprepared to face
my Maker, with succour close at hand, nerved
us all to make extraordinary exertions, and I
mentally prayed for presence of mind, for I
felt that the safety of the whole depended so

entirely on me, that I used the whole of my
breathing time in cheering up the three men
who could not swim. All eyes were fixed on
the barge close to us, and approaching rapidly,
but every now and then hid by the overhanging crest of a wave which ingulphed us a
second afterwards, keeping us down longer
and longer as our strength failed us and we
filled with water. She was almost within our
reach when a furious breaker swept her past
us with the speed of lightning, and buried us
for some seconds. How plainly I saw the faces
of all in the barge as they passed us, pale as
death, with eyes straining with eager anxiety !
but they were as helpless as ourselves, and half
filled their boat in endeavouring to round-to.
My men now began to despair, and utter the
most piercing cries, and one of them said,
" Good bye, Mr. Barnard, I am going down;"
but I tapped him on the shoulder, and told
him to look at the pinnace, not then far from
us, and we held on by the keel of the boat
with the energy and despair of drowning men.
At least six times did the surf wash me from
one end of the boat to the other, my hand

grasping the keel the whole length; still on
came our rescuers, our only hope :—some
screeched and howled, others left the boat and
swam towards the approaching one, and I
exerted my remaining strength in calling out
" Luff, luff," fearing she would pass us like the
barge; however, we were all picked up but
one poor boy, named Crapwell, who was probably taken down by a shark. I had grasped
the bight of the jib-sheet, and when hauled in
to the pinnace was quite exhausted and black
in the face, and the men were much in the
same plight. Fortunately, the Chipoli was at
anchor about three miles from us, and we received every attention and kindness from the
American officers, and Dr. Tuckerman soon
restored us with bottles of hot water at our
feet, and friction of warm blankets, and I
remained on board, sending the boats on. We
all suffered from an unquenchable thirst, and
a great soreness in our backs and limbs; however, I was able to get to work the next day.

On the 11th we observed the ship at anchor
outside, in company with a brig, which proved
to be the Defensivo, fitted as a whaler, of

which I had received previous information; and on searching her, her equipment was found so unfit for catching fish, that she was detained, and sent away in charge of Lieutenant Molesworth, to the Primeiro Islands for repair. At Quillimane I was asked if I thought it possible for her captain to be allowed to get on shore, as he was a friend of Senhor Isidore, collector of the customs. I said I would ask Captain Wyvill if they would give me his name; and as this name, Paulo Roderigue, coincided with that on the brig's papers, it was a strong proof that she was expected, and led in a great measure to her being condemned, as the captain and crew had signed a protest in which they declared that Quillimane was not their destination, and that their sole object was whaling. She had no clearance from the custom house, nor manifest, and was under Brazilian colours.

We were detained at the mouth of the river by strong south-westerly winds, until Wednesday 19th, and during the whole time experienced the hospitality of the American officers, and their kind consideration and anxiety to provide for all our wants will ever be gratefully remembered by the officers of the Cleopatra. On arriving on board and informing the captain that a number of chained slaves had been seen marching to southward, and that there was a vessel expected in that direction, I was sent away with the barge and a fortnight's provisions, and the ship sailed, and the current setting strong to the northward I could not fetch in, and preferred running through the breakers to remaining outside all night, full as we were of empty casks. We got in famously, shipping but little water, but nearly stove the dingy which was towing astern, a sea washing her nearly into the barge, and staving her; however, this was counterbalanced by my seeing the gig in which I had been capsized high up on the beach about five miles from the entrance of the river.

I took up my quarters on board the Chipoli, and the next morning at day-light pulled across and launched the gig, recovering my carpet bag, in which I had money and clothes; still my loss was severe, as my watch was ruined, and many other things spoilt, and I must have been at least £20 out of pocket.

I made occasional trips to the town, and on the 28th the Governor-General arrived from Mozambique in the Gentil Liberador, whose name I found he had changed to the Don Juan de Castro. I was looking from Azvedo's porch through a glass, and the moment I reported the Portuguese Flag at the main all was hurry and bustle; dressing gowns gave place to gold-laced coats and long beards to cut chins; thin men staggered under fat epaulets and snuff, and butter-coloured artillerymen risked their lives by firing a salute from ghosts of guns of all calibres mostly taken from wrecked slavers; and the sable inhabitants, whose dress and undress are always the same, crowded to the beach, laughing and grinning as if they were the happiest creatures in the world. I offered the services of my boat, which the Governor of Quillimane accepted, and I accompanied him on board and had an interview with the General, who is a fine affable old soldier and has crossed the line fifteen times, and seems delighted to meet with an Englishman to talk over his adventures. He was accompanied by Dr. William Peters, a Prussian physician and naturalist, on a mission from his king to collect specimens of natural curiosities for the Royal Museum, at Berlin.

The General landed on the 30th, and attended mass, after which they fired a salute, during which an artilleryman had his arm shattered, from the gun not being properly sponged, leaving a few sparks which burnt the man's thumb, who was stopping the vent, and made him withdraw it, and the charge ignited while being rammed home. The poor fellow was immediately in a blaze, but, being black, little sympathy was evinced by the bystanders, and although I had to run the gauntlet before the soldiers who were firing a *feu de joie*, I was one of the first to tear his trousers off. On examination it was found that amputation was requisite, but the surgeon had no instruments, and the tide was too low to send to the American brig for theirs, and the man would most certainly have died from loss of blood, had not Dr. Peters been there and humanely come forward, and, after searching in vain for better instruments, after a lapse of three hours performed the operation above the elbow with a carving knife and carpenter's saw, the former of which I sharpened on my boot whilst Peters prepared the latter with a file. I assisted him by holding the arm and afterwards the artery, the gentlemen of the place being in their Sunday's clothes and not accustomed to the sight of blood: the man recovered, and afterwards went to Mozambique with the General. In my interviews with the latter he expressed himself most anxious to do every thing in his power with the limited means he possessed to put a stop to the slave trade on the east coast, in evidence of which he is the only Governor-General who has visited Quillimane; and he promised to forward to us any information he might receive.

On August 4th I returned on board the ship with wood and water, leaving some casks behind me on board the Chipoli, for which I was not able to return until the 9th; a heavy swell, in which we rolled our ports under, setting right on the bar. I had a long conversation with the General, and he accepted

Captain Wyvill's invitation to accompany us to Zanzibar in the beginning of September.

I learnt that no slaves were expected for thirty or forty days, about which time one or two might be looked for at Quizungo or one of the rivers to the north of Quillimane. On May 1st Lieutenant Trou, commanding the Portuguese brig of war, boarded the Brazilian bark Julia, fitted for slaves, and detained her three days, but the Governor of Quillimane allowed her to go.

The latter end of August we went across to St. Augustine's Bay for bullocks and water, and whilst standing along the land observed two brigs at anchor in Tallear Bay, and I was despatched in the gig to board them. A long reef extends from one bay to the other, and a high piece of table-land, called Westminster Hall, serves as a mark for the passage. The first brig I boarded was French, named La Jeune, from Bourbon, collecting l'orseille, and corning beef; the other was the Prince Albert, from Mauritius for l'orseille, which is a kind of moss, producing a very beautiful scarlet dye, and is pressed into

bales, by means of a large screw, weighing
250 lbs. It is purchased by barter with powder, clouty, beads, and iron pots, the value of
one dollar and a-half purchasing fifteen dollars'
worth.

The breeze having set in strong, I took
up my quarters for the night on board the
Prince Albert, and received much civility from
M. Servais, the master, and returned in the
morning with the land breeze. The natives
crowded round the vessel the moment they
saw me arrive on board, and thought to ex-
tort about treble the usual price for their
rotten old shells, the women taking a most
prominent part in this traffic, and keeping
back the good ones in hopes of getting rid
of their trash. We had brought some of the
American corvette's powder from Quillimane
to purchase bullocks, &c., from twenty to
twenty-five pounds being the price of a beast
weighing about 350 pounds, a tumbler full, of
half-a-dozen fowls. One day, I landed with
the butcher and cooks, to superintend the
corning of two oxen, and the natives went
through all kinds of manœuvres to get beef

out of me. Nothing came amiss to them: even the entrails and hide about the heels were half cooked and devoured with voracity, cut up by their sharp spears. A more importunate set of savages cannot be imagined; buttons, beads, and fish-hooks are taken as a matter of course, without the least appearance of thanks. I took a very pretty little child on my knee, fondled her and gave her some biscuit and beef, after which I found that she was constantly employed to beg for the others, and not long after she left me, she laid her head in a woman's lap, and in a short time numerous lives were lost, and I had a strange sensation of itching all the rest of the day.

The next day I took the pinnace up to Tallear Bay, and established a market on a heap of green boughs, purchasing fowls, eggs, beans, and shells, for powder, clouty, beads, and fish-hooks; and on the 2nd of September, I sailed for Quillimane, where, after a passage of four days, we met the Lily, learnt the death of the Duke of Sussex, and the birth of the Princess. On the 7th, I left in the pinnace for the town, dingy in tow, accompanied by

Denman; and arriving at the bar at low water, found it breaking right across, but not sufficiently to endanger a large boat, so I pushed across and unfortunately a breaker filled the dingy, and capsized her, so that she acted as a drag; but being anxious to tow her into smooth water, I held on rather longer than was prudent, and a large sea boiling up put us in some danger, and the men became alarmed, so I gave the word " cut," and away we went without shipping any water, and went alongside the Chipoli, where I left Denman and four men, who, in the evening, recovered the dingy, as she floated down the river.

On arriving at the town, I found Azvedo in great trouble. It appears that his father-in-law, Moraes, had farmed a large estate, paying the rent to the Government; but as it was entailed property, and had come to the son-in-law of the Governor of Quillimane, he demanded the arrears of rent, which were refused, pending an appeal to the Supreme Court at Goa, against a judgment passed at Quillimane. On this, high words ensued, and the Governor called out the military, and surrounded the house, planting two pieces of artillery before the door, and enforced the payment, taking at the same time 170 stand of arms from the stores, thus using his power as Governor to carry out his private ends. I took charge of papers, detailing the whole affair, for the Governor-General, and returned to the brig, where I again experienced the hospitality of our kind American friends until the 11th, when we managed to cross just before it broke. I had now received so many lessons that I determined to run no more risks, particularly as I had just heard that the poor pilot, who first received me at Quillimane, had, with all his boat's crew, been found dead on the beach, his launch having capsized : this man had been going in and out in all weathers for many years.

CHAPTER III.

LEAVING the Lily off Quillimane, we started for Mozambique, on September 11, and arrived on the 14th. The following morning I accompanied the captain to wait on his Excellency, the Governor-General, and arranged that he should embark with suite, and Dr. Peters, for Zanzibar, on the 18th. In the meantime we had an opportunity of seeing the city and its inhabitants.

The palace was formerly a Jesuit convent, and bears evident traces of the good fathers having taken care of themselves; large and airy rooms, good kitchens, and gardens, affording all the requisites for a comfortable residence. The hospital, a fine building, was also a convent, and the whole place shows plainly that, at a former period, its streets must have been crowded with merchants and the produce of many countries ; now, it is all falling into ruins, and house after house seems to be crumbling away; and one cannot help feeling how just is the doom of a place whose merchants flourished by trafficking in the flesh of their fellow creatures, who are even now considered by them as belonging more to the brute than the human species.

One of the aides-de-camp gave us a soirée, where we met three or four well-dressed ladies : they were attended by their slaves, little black girls, rigged out with a profusion of ornaments and jewellery, without whom they never move. We invited them on board the ship the next day and they seemed to be much pleased. They appear to have no education, and speak only an execrable kind of Portuguese picked up from the negresses, who are their constant and almost only companions until they are married. Their dowry consists of houses and slaves, and sometimes an estate

across the water. By law a man cannot hold
property there without residing on it, a regu-
lation which was formerly very strictly carried
out for the purpose of increasing the white
population as much as possible.

The Banyans form a great proportion of
the inhabitants of Mozambique, in fact they
are scattered all over the Portuguese possessions, and are the principal merchants, agents,
and bankers, in these places. They were formerly driven from their country by the Mar-
hattas, and placed themselves under the protection of the Portuguese flag,* which then flew
triumphant in the Indian seas, and removed
with their families and goods to Diu in such
numbers, that they were obliged to burrow
and make an immense number of habitations
under ground. They believe in metempsy-
chosis, and therefore eat nothing that has life,

* They were first driven from Cambaia to Guzarrate
and Mecca, and from thence came to Diu and Damas,
where, at the end of the 17th century, they founded a
Company with very extensive privileges of commerce
on the East Coast of Africa, and although these ceased
in the middle of the 18th century, they still hold the
commerce almost exclusively.

or kill even noxious animals. The name Banian imports, in the Brahmin language, innocent and harmless—void of all guile. They are so gentle that they cannot endure to see either a fly or a worm injured; and when struck they will patiently bear it, without resisting or returning the blow. Their dress consists of a long white robe descending to their ankles, a large turban arranged in smooth narrow folds. Altogether they present a most effeminate appearance. In buying and selling, these people never use words: one of them looses his girdle and spreads it on his knee, under this the buyer and seller place their hands. When the seller takes the buyer's whole hand it denotes a thousand, as many times as he squeezes it as many thousands; five fingers denote five hundred; one finger one hundred; half a finger, to second joint, fifty; the small end of the finger ten. The cant term of "Banyan day" amongst sailors takes its origin from the above, as on this day they have no meat.

On Tuesday, the 19th of September, we sailed for Zanzibar, and arrived on the 25th.

The passage to the anchorage is intricate, but the water is clear and with a leading wind the shoals are easily avoided. We anchored about a third of a mile off the town, and saluted the red flag of the Imaun of Muscat, which was returned by the King of the Seas, a large sixty-gun frigate, whose moorings have not been lifted for eleven years. Our Consul, Captain Hammerton, came off immediately, and wrote to His Highness to know when it would be convenient for him to receive the Governor-General. The answer was, that he would be ready about three or four hours after sunrise the next morning, their time being always reckoned in that way.

General Lima left the ship under a salute, and we all accompanied him in full tog, and were received at the palace by the Imaun's sons and friends, each giving us a shake by the hand as they passed us along the line, like firebuckets, to His Highness, who conducted us in person to the audience-chamber, a long barn of a place with a marble floor, and walls that had been whitewashed once, but were now variegated with cobwebs and dust. Chairs were placed all

E

round this princely apartment, and we were
seated in rows like stuck pigs, and the coun-
cillors, relations, and favourites, kicked off
their sandals and filled the vacant seats.

The conversation was carried on through
Captain Hammerton and an interpreter, and
consisted of very anxious inquiries after each
other's healths, and assurances on the part of
His Highness that the island was the Governor-
General's during his stay, and that every thing
we required should be sent off. The Captain
said that we merely wanted a few bullocks,
and six were sent off the following morning.
On taking our leave we were invited to dine
with His Highness at three the next day.

Never was a man so falsely represented or
so little understood as this petty Prince. In
England we hear of his munificence, his power,
his men-of-war, his presents of line of battle
ships, and fancy him a great potentate,
whereas he is merely upheld in his shadow of authority by the countenance of the
English. His ships are dismantled and rot-
ting at their anchors; sailors he has none.
His palace (so called) is a ramshackle old

building, a part of which fell in some time
since and killed two of his wives, so that he
has only seventy-three left. A Banyan farms
the customs-revenue, and his whole income
from all his possessions is not more than
£100,000 per annum.

The following day we were punctual to the
dinner hour, and found the table groaning
under the substantial things of this world. A
goat roasted whole, and a hind quarter of
beef, were the top and bottom dishes, and
mountainous pillaus, with sweetmeats of many
sorts surrounding their bases, left very little
room for the glasses, &c. Decanters were scattered about with sherbet, tasting strongly of
rosewater. The Imaun was seated near the
table, and his principal officers and attendants
waited on us, many of them speaking English:
they never eat with Christians; and their Ramazan having just commenced, it must have been
not a little tantalizing for them to look on.
The Ramazan lasts for thirty days, during which
time nothing passes their lips between sunrise
and sunset, not even a drop of water; but they
make up for lost time in the night, having two

meals, the second at three o'clock, when a gun fires to announce to all true Believers that it is time to lay in a stock for the day.

The trade is carried on by vessels with one immense sail : they are commonly known by the name of Dows, but, properly called, Bungalows. Some of these coast along and go into every nook and corner on the coast of Africa, collecting ivory, gum, copal, and slaves; the trade in the latter is very brisk, and these boats will carry from three to four hundred. As we were standing in to the anchorage, there were one ahead and one astern of us full of them. There is a regular slave-market, and the purchasers pay a dollar a-head duty to the collector of customs. They appear happy and contented, and their condition appears to be much better than in their own country. They have two days in the week to themselves, and not much to do on the other days, and in their present degraded state, "nothing to do and bask in the sun" is nigger's paradise.

During the north-east monsoon, hundreds of these bungalows come from the Red Sea and Persian Gulf, bringing carpets, rugs, coffee, and the produce of all the places in these seas. They have nothing but a compass, and but very few of them have any idea of taking observations, making sure of a fair wind and coasting it along. Should they meet with a foul wind, they smoke their pipes and trust in God to take them somewhere; and many find themselves in the bottom of the Red, or adjacent seas, with valuable cargoes of ivory, and gum-copal. We found two American and one English house established at Zanzibar; of the two former, one is the Consul's, named Waters; the other is that of a Mr. Webb, formerly master of a merchant-vessel. From the latter I got specimens of the gum-copal which is found on the coast of Africa and Zanzibar, in districts void of trees. It must be formed very quickly, as I have a lump in which may be seen wasps, cockroaches, and various kinds of insects.

Captain Hammerton complained that he had no flag-staff, so I was sent on shore and rigged one on the top of his house, and had the honour of hoisting the English flag for the first time. The Imaun frigate saluted it with twenty-one guns, and it caused much jealousy

amongst those who had, until lately, the mono-
poly of trade, and have now a presentiment
that John Bull having now got his foot in, will
soon squeeze in his whole body.

. When Captain Hammerton first arrived, an
Englishman could not walk the streets without
being insulted, and one of the chief men having
done something very glaring, he insisted that
the Imaun should have him publicly flogged,
which of course caused a great sensation, and
His Highness offered him the lives of three
slaves instead, but in the end complied with
the original demand, and had the offender well
paid off in the market-place.   Since then the
sons of burnt fathers dare no longer laugh at
an Englishman's beard.

- A short time previous to our arrival a
French brig-of-war had been there from Bourbon, and made a treaty with the Imaun,
which allows the French to hire as labourers
the subjects of His Highness: there is also a
clause permitting slaves to be hired, provided
the price of their freedom is paid, and that
they are willing to go for a certain number of
years; and if the stipulations which are to be

entered into by both parties are strictly acted
up to, the condition of Darky will be considerably improved, as he may eventually return to
his own country with a sum of money and a
trade, and perhaps this may be one of the best
means of commencing civilization in Africa—
without which the slave trade never can be put
down, with all England's sacrifice of life and
treasure.

The town of Zanzibar is an intricate kind
of labyrinth, the streets so narrow that two
can scarcely walk abreast, and so short and
winding that, without a guide, the only chance
of getting out of them is making direct for
the beach, along which they are beginning to
build large stone houses; and in a few years
the increase of trade in European and American hands will make a vast improvement. But
the government is so despotic, that the lower
orders must necessarily remain in a most degraded state. When the Imaun gives an
entertainment, he sends his servants to the
market-place, and these take whatever they
want for the service of His Highness, without
the least payment, whatever be the circum-

stances of the persons they rob. The Banyans
drive a regular trade in shells and mats, asking strangers double and treble their value;
but there is a great variety. On the 30th we
left the anchorage, and worked to the southward between the isle and the main, seeing the
English ensign long after the other flags had
become invisible. May our clever and jolly Consul live to make it respected for many years, and
give our merchants reason to bless the day when
he erected the "Father of Flagstaffs."

On the 6th of October we made Comoro,
and were detained off it for several days by
light winds, calms, and currents, and did not
arrive at Johanna until the 13th. Comoro,
though nominally under the authority of the
King of Johanna, is divided amongst a number
of petty chiefs, who live independently of each
other, who are constantly fighting, and who
pay no revenue. They have a great number
of cattle, which they send in droves to
Johanna, where, from the frequent visits of
ships, they meet with a good market.

Johanna is a most picturesque and beautiful
island, covered with cocoa-nut, bananas, date,

and a great variety of the palm-tree, on the sides and tops of mountains, rising one behind the other in constant succession, until the highest peak reaches the height of 5,900 feet. The water is deep within a quarter of a mile of the beach, and from the ship it appears quite close before the anchor is let go, when the canoes, supported by an outrigger on each side, crowd round with the produce of the island, consisting of pine-apples, bananas, plantains, cocoa-nuts, sweet potatoes, and arrowroot. Two of the King's principal officers came off to wait on the Captain, dressed in a profusion of gold-lace and vests of gay colours; they wore also handsomely mounted swords, and seemed to be on excellent terms with themselves.

The King complained to the Captain and Governor-General, when they waited on His Majesty, that Said Hamza, one of the ministers of late King Alloy, had purchased a barque at the Mauritius, and called at Bourbon to endeavour to get the Governor to assist him in getting possession of the throne, promising, that if he succeeded he would allow

E 3

the French to establish themselves at Johanna, Mohilla, and Comoro; and the following sentence was found in the Governor of Bourbon's letter to the King: "I have been perfectly satisfied with the wisdom of the words of your envoy, and with the way in which he has defended your interests in the face of the re-clamations of your competitor, Said Hamza." On this was founded a charge of high treason, and the Captain offered to assist the Sultan in carrying the law into execution. Consequently, I was sent the next morning to take possession of the barque Vrai Français, and seize her papers; after which I accompanied the Captain and Governor-General on shore; and after a palaver in a private room, (the entrance to which was so narrow that we were obliged to work in edgeways), the three judges were sent for, and a court assembled in the audience-chamber, round which the accusers, accused, judges and friends, sat indiscrimi-nately, the King being on a sofa between the Governor-General and Captain, with an inter-preter before them.

The first part of the business was to make the

accused prisoner, a proceeding they did not at
all understand, allowing him to retain his sword,
until it was pointed out by the Captain, and he
was then marched off between two constables
in white shifts, and wands of the same colour in
their hands. In about a quarter of an hour
the court was opened and the prisoner brought
forward. He was decidedly the most intel-
ligent-looking man of the whole, and his fine
handsome countenance, and long gray beard.
gave him quite a venerable appearance, as he
took his seat on a sofa next to the judges.
The evidence against him was given by two
young Arabs, who had been present when he
spoke to the Governor of Bourbon, and swore
that he had asked for soldiers to place him on
the throne, &c. On being called upon for
his defence, he commenced, in very good
English, a long account of his two years' residence, and of his going to Bourbon for papers
for his vessel, when the Governor proposed
to him to take possession of the throne.
But he was cut short in the middle of his
yarn, found guilty, and his property confis-
cated; and the court broke up. After which

the King walked arm in arm with the Captain down to the beach, followed by a numerous train, amongst whom was Said Hamza as cool as if nothing had happened. I was then sent to deliver up the barque and her papers to an officer sent by the King.

That same evening we sailed for Mayotta, leaving Dr. Peters to prosecute his researches at Johanna; and on the 17th ran through the Bandeli passage, which is about three-quarters of a mile broad, between reefs under water, which can be seen perfectly well from the clearness of the water; and an excellent mark put up by the French takes you in easily enough; and, when once inside, it is the most perfect harbour that can be imagined, quite land-locked, and protected by reefs from all winds. I was sent to wait on Captain Passo, the Governor, whom I found in a small building, between a hut and a cottage, but very tastefully fitted up. The French had been settled there four years, for the purpose of recruiting invalids from Nos Beh, where the mortality is ten per cent. per annum; but they find Mayotta very unhealthy, and during

the rainy months, January, February, and
March, the people are all sickly, and the rain
never ceases for a single day. They have as
yet no fortifications, but about eighty soldiers.

The natives are a mixture of Arabs, Johannese, and Sacalavas from Madagascar—the
latter having been brought over by different
chiefs from Bembatooka, who have at different times been driven from their own country,
and taken possession of Mayotta, until obliged to leave by a superior force. Raminitoe
and Ransouli were the last two adventurers:
the former we expelled from Mohilla in
1830, in the Jaseur, and the latter gave up
the island to the French, claiming it by right
of conquest; but the Johanna Sultan still
asserts his right to it. The Governor told
me that, when the French first arrived, there
was not a bullock nor fowl on the island, and
that they had burnt each other's crops in all
directions. Now they appear to be improv-
ing, and to be surrounded with stock; but
the watering-place for ships is in a stream
among mud and mangrove bushes, the certain
prognostics of fever and disease.

On the 19th we sailed, and passed just outside the passage a French store-ship and corvette going in, the former for the soldiers and sick. On the 21st we again anchored at Johanna, and I was sent to the King with a document signed by the Governor-General and Captain, certifying that the trial of Said Hamza had been fairly conducted in their presence. I also got from the King a statement, in Arabic, of the proposition of the Governor of Bourbon, which was, to allow him to establish an hospital at Johanna for the sick from Nos Beh and Mayotta, and to keep soldiers there to guard them. For this the Governor would pay a stipulated sum, and *perhaps* assist him in getting possession of Mohilla and Comoro. The King's answer was, that he could not comply with their request to allow them to establish an hospital, but that he would always afford every facility should a ship wish to land any sick.

The Johannese, in general, seem to hold the French in great dread, and to place great dependence on the English; but they are such consummate hypocrites, and so accustomed to the use of "soft soap" from their infancy, that there is no believing them—their whole aim is to make money by getting to the blind side of strangers. They are hospitable, however, in their own houses; and Dr. Peters experienced much kindness, living at his Majesty's, and making excursions all over the island, which he describes as most beautiful and interesting. He astonished the natives not a little by walking for fourteen successive hours to and from a lake in the interior, which he found covered with ducks; and the surrounding trees swarmed with birds of most magnificent plumage. This place is held sacred, and nothing allowed to be killed there; pilgrimages are made to it, and it is considered three days' journey from Dermonic, the town; and there are villages at the distance from each other of two hours' walk, the inhabitants of which are very civil.

The Johannese are nearly Arab, and follow strictly the forms of the Mahometan religion. The Ramazan is kept by them; and on one occasion, on going into the King's house, he was at his devotions, which he performed with

great activity. He had just finished his ablu-
tions, and appeared in the audience-chamber
in a long chemise reaching to the ground,
jumped on a sofa, held his hands up, and
prostrated himself over and over again. After
this, the sun having dipped, he commenced
eating betel-nut with great avidity.

Their women are carefully shut up from the
eyes of strangers; but the curiosity of the
fair sex will not be baulked here more than in
any other part of the globe, and various are
their manœuvres to see a white man. The
Doctor was frequently invited to enter a house,
and found himself placed in a strong light,
whilst tittering and laughing in an adjoining
dark apartment shewed that there were more
eyes than one on him, and presents of neck-
laces made of sweet-smelling flowers were sent
out to him. The interpreter told him also,
that the ladies had taken a great fancy to
him—" he had such a nice long nose."

The King was anxious to have a prescription
for the Queen, whose complaint he described to
the Doctor, who said that it was necessary
for him to see her. He was accordingly

ushered into the room, and found her dressed in a profusion of gay ornaments, such as bangles, rings, ear-rings, &c. Her face was closely veiled, but she managed very dexterously to show it for an instant, and then leant on the King's shoulder;—this one, I believe, is the favourite of *the four*. On taking my leave, His Majesty presented me with a spice necklace, as a small mark of his friendship, and said that he hoped soon to see me in command of a ship. That evening we sailed for Mozambique, and arrived on the 26th of October, and landed the Governor-General, whose departure we all much regretted, for his habitual good humour and amusing anecdote passed away many an hour pleasantly, which would have been otherwise cheerless and dreary. The next day we sailed for Majunga, where it was alleged, in a letter from the Comoro Islands, that the English flag had been insulted.

On October 30th we anchored off the town of Majunga, in Bembatooka Bay, and I was sent to the Governor to demand an explanation of the alleged insult. On landing, I met an American named Marks, who had resided there for many years, collecting hides and tallow, and I learnt from him the following information: In the beginning of the year a Monsieur Bonifait had sailed from the Mauritius in the English barque Sampson, with a general cargo for the east coast of Africa, and west coast of Madagascar; at Majunga he found a Portuguese named Renaud Leseppes, speaking the Malagaihe language, apparently a likely agent to make a good profit on the merchandize. Consequently goods to the value of 9000 dollars were intrusted to him; and in July the vessel came back for a return, and commenced shipping rice, ebony, hides, tallow, and bees'-wax, when, all at once, the supply was stopped, and M. Bonifait was induced to disembark a quantity of goods which the Ovas promised to pay for in Spanish dollars, as they wanted to send some cloth to Tenenerivo the capital; but no sooner were they in possession of the merchandize than they declared that it was not even enough to pay for what had been embarked—that Renaud had paid for nothing, nor did they recognize

him in the transaction. This led to an angry
discussion: the workmen struck, leaving sundry
casks of salt beef on the beach; the captain
and supercargo were made prisoners, and the
soldiers sent off to take out that part of the
cargo which they say was not paid for. Bonifait managed in the mean time to get to Nos
Beh in a canoe, and the French Governor
said, that if the lives of British subjects were
in danger, he would send a man-of-war; if not,
he could not interfere.

Having learnt this much I worked my way
up the hill leading to the fort, the gate of
which was guarded by two Ova sentries, who
blocked the entrance by crossing their muskets, holding their spears in their other hand.
An officer from the Governor passed me
through this as well as two other gates
guarded in the same manner, and I was received by his Excellency at the door of his
house, with a guard of sixty soldiers, and a
roll on the drums. He was dressed in a blue
surtout, unwhisperables to match, and a yellow waistcoat, and after I had explained the
cause of our visit, through an interpreter, he

assured me that far from wishing to insult the
English flag, he had been most anxious to set
things to rights, but that the ship had sailed
suddenly and would not return, although he
kept dipping and hoisting his flag to her as a
signal, until she disappeared, and placed the
goods left behind in a store under lock and
key.

I told him that the Captain would wait
upon him if he would return his visit, but he
said he never went on board, "makee the too
much sick in de head." I asked him what
number of guns he would like to be saluted
with, and he preferred seven to nine, as it
would be less expense in returning it. He then
offered us a bullock in the Queen's name, and
had tumblers and liqueurs put on the table.

Civilization has made great strides amongst
the Ovas, and under a good government much
might be done for them, for even now the
good effects of Radama's short reign are not
yet extinguished, notwithstanding the savage
bigotry of the present Queen. A few of them
write a good hand taught them by the mis- .
sionaries, and form altogether a great contrast

to the St. Augustine's Bay people, who are perfect savages.

· The officers in attendance on the Governor were dressed in most indescribable uniforms: generals, aides-de-camp, militiamen, and all kinds of corps had contributed something to each, and some of them would make famous figures for a Cruikshank, looking so awkwardly stiff that it was quite laughable to look at them, the perspiration pouring off them in streams. On leaving the Fort, I was accosted by the Colonel, who had been a boy on board the Jaseur with me; he seemed quite delighted at meeting his old shipmate, and took me by the hand, saying, "What! see him again! eh! after long time, him too glad!" I took him on board, gave him some clothes, and to shew his gratitude he cheated me as much as he could in the purchase of bullocks, for which I paid eleven dollars each. The getting these beasts into the boats was the most laughable and exciting sight I have seen for a long time. In a yard, the entrance to which was a passage through a house, were about forty oxen, from which we were to take our choice. A

Black placing a rope over the horns of the one I pointed out, this is led through the passage, and about fourteen clapped on outside, drag him out; the moment he gets through he gives a snort, and rushes furiously at those nearest to him; but the rope being well manned it is gradually shortened in and a turn taken round the stern of an old Dow. This process infuriates the savage animal, which paws the ground, snuffs the air, and seems extremely anxious to make his horns better acquainted with his enemies, at whom he at last makes a rush, is brought up all standing, and falls on his beam ends, when he is overpowered by numbers, lashed, and bundled into the boat; now and then they break adrift and give us a regular hunt, which causes much fun.

The town of Bembatooka is well up the bay, and not frequented by ships, but stock of different kinds comes down in boats. As well as Majunga, it was under the dominion of the Sacalavas, until about twenty years ago, when Adriantsolo or Ransouli was driven out by Raminitoc, the brother of Radama, who was in his turn obliged to fly to save his own head; for it is no joke offending the higher powers in this island, who merely give the option of "poison or decapitation," and the sentences are executed with most barbarous cruelty, and are of a nature too sickening to relate.

Christianity is forbidden under pain of death, although in Radama's time it had made considerable progress. Not a month before we arrived at this place, the brother of the secretary of the Governor was killed, cut up in pieces, and distributed to the surrounding houses as a warning, for having been found exercising some of the forms of Christianity. Their religion seems to be a mixture of barbarous superstitions, as they worship the bones of the dead, and place implicit reliance in charms. One of their most horrid customs is the trial by poison. If a person is suspected of harbouring any design against the Queen, or if a man suspects his wife, they administer a poison on a bit of fowl's-skin, and watch its operation. If the person is innocent they suppose that the skin will be

thrown up without harming the accused, but
should it prove fatal, it is taken as a sure sign
of guilt. About a year or more since, the Queen
sent to Port Dauphin for some singing girls,
who had all to undergo this fiery ordeal, and
one poor girl remained in a most dreadful
state for a long time, and was left on the
beach to die, her mother watching her from as
near a spot as she dared; and at last the poor
creature got rid of the fowl's-skin and begged
her mother to run to the Governor, to say she
was innocent, who immediately sent down soldiers to beat out her brains on the spot, as it
had remained down so long.

From Majunga we went to Nos Beh, an
island near the north-west end of Madagascar,
where the French have made a kind of settlement. On anchoring, I was sent to wait on the
Governor, and found him living in a kind of
cock-loft, not half as roomy as the generality
of signal stations, his bed-room, eating-room,
and sitting-room being all in one over a dirty
little place full of muskets and cooking uten-
sils. His name is Morell, a captain of artillery:
he was very polite, and after a long chat I

took my leave, saying that the Captain would
be glad to salute the French flag, if it could
be returned from the shore, which was done
from two field pieces. They seem to have made
but little progress in their establishment in
the four years they have been there. No guns
are mounted, no stone houses built, and the
hospitals, which were built on a hill on high
piles, proved so unhealthy that they have been
removed, and the soldiers, who are not above
thirty in number, live on board the Leone, a
small corvette fitted for the purpose. There
is a small mountain opposite the Governor's,
named the "Devil's Mountain," from the circumstance of every soul having died who was
employed to bring stones from it for building
a small jetty, and it is to be feared that the
climate will prevent any European Power from
making use of one of the most beautiful har-
bours in the world.

Deep in the bay is the Arab village, where
stock of all descriptions can be obtained at a
very cheap rate. I went there to look for
an agent of the barque Sampson, and found
a M. Monclar, a native of Bourbon, left by

F

Bonifait to dispose of a quantity of merchandize. From him I learnt sufficient of the
Majunga affair to induce me to take him on
board to the Captain, as well as a Portuguese
of the name of Camache, from whom Renaud
had stolen 3,000 dollars in the following way :
At Mozambique Senhor Camache had met
Renaud, who being a plausible kind of bird,
induced him to advance 1,200 dollars, for
which he was to receive ten per cent. in a few
months at Bembatooka. On arriving there
he found no effects, and was induced by a
plausible excuse not only to allow his goods
to be kept, but to pay a further advance of
940 dollars on a bill of Renaud's, whom he
accompanied to Noussourangue, from whence
he was to cross the Island of Madagascar to
Antongil Bay, where Renaud represented
that he had a large establishment. On the
road he fell sick, and intrusting the remainder
of his goods, making the whole amount advanced 3,000 dollars, he found that he had
been humbugged and robbed, that there was
no establishment, and that his friend had left
him in the lurch, after attempting to poison

him; for all the fowls in the hut died after taking what he threw on the ground, from its suspicious appearance. For three years after this M. Camache heard nothing of his companion, when, on the arrival of the Sampson at Nos Beh, he learnt that he was at Noussourangue, and immediately volunteered his services as pilot to that place, where they had a most affectionate interview, Renaud falling on his knees, and calling himself a poor wretch, swearing that he would pay him the half of his profits on Bonifait's affairs. After this they commenced shipping rice, ebony, tallow, and bees'-wax; and when a certain quantity was on board, they found that the Bembatooka farce had been acted over again, and that M. Renaud had paid for nothing, and M. Bonifait getting warm on the subject, the Governor threw a bottle at his head, and made him and his captain prisoners, sending soldiers off to take out the ebony and bees'-wax. With this information we sailed for Rafala Bay, at the entrance of which is Noussourangue, an Ova fort. We took with us both Monclar and Camache to identify the villain, and anchored

off the town the following day about three
miles from the shore, and I was sent to wait
upon the Governor, accompanied by Denman
and Lehenson. He lives in the fort about
three miles from the landing-place, the first
half over a most beautiful plain covered with
verdure and green shrubs, the other up as
steep a hill as a fat man could wish to meet
in a tropical climate. On my way up I met
a Portuguese, whom I recognized as a Quillimane acquaintance, and found that it was the
man I was in quest of. He had been branded
in the forehead by the captain of a merchant-
vessel with a "V" for "Voleur" for one of his
tricks, and he had a hang-dog appearance,
sufficient, one would imagine, to put anybody
on his guard.

On arriving at the fort we were received by
the Governor, dressed in surtout-coat and
epaulets, and a gold-lace cocked-hat, a large
guard presenting arms and three drums kick-
ing up a most horrible din. He seemed in a
great fright about the Sampson affair, and
most anxious to prove that the fault was not
on his side, and I recommended him to send

off Renaud to explain matters, but it was not until the next day that I got him on board, and the captain detained him as prisoner and went on shore. The Governor sent a litter for him, but he preferred walking; however, they would insist on his being carried into the fort, and his weight made them grunt not a little. His sable Excellency abused Renaud for all the misunderstandings, and declared that he had cheated them as well as every body else.

After this we returned to Nos Beh, and, on the passage, the Captain said it was necessary for Monclar and Camache to go with us to Mozambique to bring charges against Renaud, on which a violent dispute arose between them, each declaring he would not go, so we hauled our wind and threatened to take them both, when the French put on a savage countenance, walked up to the Portuguese, and pronounced "Un coup de pistolet finera tout cela," and Camache immediately came to terms and consented to go, so we landed. Monclar and I accompanied him to the Arab village, where I bought three bullocks, a cow and a calf, and three calves for thirty dollars, and a great deal of rice, at the rate of 125 lbs. for one dollar. During the harvest in April and May some hundreds of Dows flock to Nos Beh from Zanzibar and other places for rice, and they say that 300 or more vessels of 300 tons each might load every year, paying only one dollar for 230 lbs.

The whole country has been very thickly wooded, but the Sacalavas have been clearing and burning in all directions, and the sides of the mountains are planted with rice, which is of two kinds, one growing in the high lands, the other in low marshy ground, one crop being ripe before the other.

CHAPTER IV.

ON the 16th November we again anchored
at Mozambique and landed our prisoner, who
was sent by the Governor to the fort, with
the intention of making him a soldier, and
sending him to Senna or Tete. The Captain
accepted an invitation to accompany the
General to Cabaceira, where his country-house
is. I accompanied them, and we were received
and entertained on the opposite side by Senhor
Cardoza, a coloured man and collector of customs, and the following day made an excursion
into the country in machilas, each having four
bearers, fine, sleek, symmetrical-looking fellows.

They generally go on at a round trot, sometimes singing in their peculiar style, jumbling apparently a vast number of words together and then giving a howl or grunt. These conveyances are remarkably easy, and you may either recline at full length or sit up shaded by a broad awning with side stops to trim it. Still the idea of being carried by slaves doing the work of beasts of burden destroys all pleasure: they, however, seem happy enough and to do it willingly, particularly as they know English officers always pay them well, which is quite contrary to the rules and customs of the Portuguese, who would persuade one that they do not know the difference between a dollar and a penny, and that fifty pounds more or less on their shoulders make very little difference,—but poor darky knows when he is the right side of the hedge as well as pale-face.

We went through several fine estates, covered with mango and cashew trees, the former so loaded with fruit that the branches in some places were broken down with the weight. The latter is a curious-looking fruit, a large nut in the shape of an ear forming first, and on the end of this a large reddish pulpy fruit, which is refreshing but very astringent in flavour. From it is distilled a very strong spirit which the Blacks are very fond of, and their leisure time is employed in getting drunk on this execrable stuff, which is quite maddening. I tasted it from the still, and could not get the disgusting flavour out of my mouth for hours. The nut is full of essential oil, and the least touch excoriates the skin; but when roasted in the ashes it is most delicious, all the oil evaporating. Two or three Portuguese gentlemen are cultivating their property to a great extent, and have already done quite enough to shew that anything will come forward, and that the only thing that is wanted is a market for the commodities.

A company has been formed at Lisbon to carry on the trade on the east coast of Africa, and they have already a capital of one million; but as yet they have not been able to acquire the requisite privileges from their Government. They want to have the power of buying sixty vessels and not to be restricted to Portuguese bottoms, and to be able to nominate and pay their own Governors. This indeed would be a blow to the slave trade, as it would open new sources of commerce, and produce new interests; and the poor wretches who are now driven from the interior like herds of cattle would be employed carrying gum-copal, ivory, gold dust, and various other articles with which Africa abounds. During the floods occasioned by the rainy season coals might be got from Tete in any quantity, and the mighty power of steam be employed in sowing the seeds of civilization, which can never be done whilst the merchants, agents, and their Governors find it, or think it, their interest to keep the Blacks in such a degraded and ignorant state, that they look upon slavery as a blessing, and voluntarily sell themselves and families for three pieces of cloth.

The coffee-trees were in full blossom, and scented the whole country. They were without leaves, and the flowers either white or pink. The berry has a strong aromatic flavour, and is preferred by many to the Mocha coffee, although few like it at first. Many fine estates are in ruins, the houses gradually crumbling away; and a few wretched huts with their sable inhabitants idly basking in the sun, or preparing their scanty fare, are the only remaining signs of what the place once was, the orange, citron and lemon-trees, and pine-apples growing amongst weeds and fallen branches. On the road, we espied a snake in the act of killing a lizard, which it had seized by the back of the neck; and as it was twining itself round the body, the General gave him a crack with his stick, and I finished his business by pulling him out of a hole by his tail, and breaking his back. I then hung him on a stick and carried him to Dr. Peters to put into spirits.

We dined at Senhor Cardoza's. His wife and daughter sat down with us, the latter a fat, round-faced, bright-eyed, good-natured, dumpy little body, as black as the ace of spades. Her name was Minina Domingo, and I talked away with her in bad Portuguese, and we soon got good friends; and in the evening hearing a great clapping of hands and singing outside, I went out and joined a dance with all the female part of our company, and about

twenty negresses, and soon made such a row
in the kitchen with a hand-organ and singing,
that nearly all the visitors came out and enjoyed the fun very much. After this we played
"old bachelor," and I persuaded them to sing,
the burden of the chorus being "Ita bons In-
glezes," soft soap having found its way to
Mozambique as well as Sam Slick's clocks, one
of which may be seen in every house, with a
fine drawing underneath, representing a farm-
house with a tree growing out of the top of
it, the house standing on the heads of a very
stiff lady and gentleman. On the following
day we went on board to divine service, and
the tide being out, we had to walk over
about two miles of a sandy flat, the captain
taking off his shoes and stockings, and shewing the example, in preference to being carried
in a machila. However, we found it no joke
in a broiling sun.

The Governor-General invited us all to a
grand hunt on the Tuesday following, and
sent out to the adjacent free tribes, to surround a place well known as abounding in
game, with nets. On the appointed day, we

left early for an estate belonging to a Moor,
visiting the port of Conducia on the way, and
at about ten sat down to a sumptuous breakfast, and the chiefs of the different tribes
came to pay their respects to the Governor.
We were all on the tiptoe of expectation, anti-
cipating fine sport, but were much disappointed
at finding it a very tame affair; for instead of
sallying with dogs and guns, and knocking
over the game as it passed us, we were expected to sit still in the house, whilst the
blacks ensnared a few unfortunate gazelles
and partridges. I went out to try to shoot
a few birds, but the burning tropical sun soon
drove me back, tired and exhausted.

We again dined at Cardoza's, for the Governor's salary is so limited, that he has not adequate means to keep up the dignity of his position, and all the people around him are better
able to entertain than himself. With his pre-
decessors it has not been so, who have generally amassed large fortunes by peculation, and
connivance at the slave trade, but General De
Lima seems to be too straightforward an old
soldier to compromise his honour, and yet

manages to entertain sufficiently to show his
good will and attachment to the English.

On November 23rd, we left our old friend,
and running along the coast between the
Primeiro Islands and the Main, arrived off
Quillimane on the 25th, and boarded a brig
named the "Flora D'Inhamban." In fact very
few vessels enter this river without being
boarded by "the frigate" as they call us, and
whom they dread very much, knowing as they
do that I can get information. of all their
movements. The next morning I went to the
town in the barge, and found that my friend
Azvedo was from home, so I took possession
of his house, ordered the cook to get dinner,
and in the evening he returned and gave me
a hearty welcome.

I learnt that a schooner had sailed with
450 slaves since our departure: they were
said to have been shipped by the Governor
Fernando, who was on a sick bed and obliged to appoint a deputy to do his duty.
An American barque named the Lucy Penniman, had been at the town with a cargo
of cloth, &c., and left an agent for the pur-

pose of purchasing slaves, and in about two months, from three to four vessels might be expected from Rio, the first to take in a cargo at the third river from Quillimane, which is called the Mariangoma, the next at the Orlinda, the next to south of Quillimane, where the Curlew once took a schooner, and the others will go wherever they think the coast is clear of men of war, and the trade is as brisk as ever. The above information I picked up bit by bit, and remained a whole day on purpose; but I was so closely watched that I could not ask half that I wished, and on the 29th got on board half roasted, having had to beat down against a fresh breeze the whole way.

On November 30th, 1843, we started for the Cape of Good Hope, and little did I think what good fortune was in store for us, when in the afternoon, it being my watch, two sail were reported ahead at anchor, a brig and a schooner, off the northern Zambozi. As we approached, we observed them interchanging signals, and two large boats leave them and run in for the land. I first boarded the brig, and found her quite deserted, with a slave-deck

laid and loaded with slave provisions. She
was well found, rigging new and in capital
order, and royal yards across. Fourteen pigs
were running about the decks, and the coops
had from six to eight dozen fowls in them. In
the cabin every thing was turned topsy-turvy,
and the numerous broken bottles and glasses,
shewed that they had strengthened the inward
man before starting. Her papers, charts,
chronometer and colours, had all disappeared,
but I recognized her as my old friend the Anna,
where I had slept several nights at Quillimane,
when she was under American colours.

Leaving a midshipman and two men on
board, I went to the brigantine and found her
much in the same state with one man only on
board. Her name was the Atala, apparently an
old vessel and not half as well found as the
brig. Still she was safe and had lots of stock,
and the next day I was ordered to take the
brig to the Cape, and to keep company with
the schooner, of which Lehenson, a Swedish
mid in our service, took charge. We lost
sight of the ship the first night, and stood
well to the eastward until the 2nd, when we

put our heads to the southward, and on the
3rd, during a calm, I sent my boat for Lehenson and Law to dine, and made arrangements about signals and keeping company.
I also supplied them with a top-gallant studding-sail, and all the following week we kept
pretty close, and occasionally spoke each other
to compare reckonings. Not having a chronometer, I constructed a current chart from
my log, which I found of great service, the
direction almost invariably proving correct.
On searching the hold I found two large bags
of slave-shackles, and sundry good things of
this world, such as a cask of wine, salt fish, preserves, bottled porter, and casks of olives, and
on the 10th Lehenson again dined with me.

I was much surprised on the 12th at
making the land; but when I got my latitude
at noon and the direction of the current on the
chart, I found that I had been drifted ninety-
eight miles in twenty-four hours, which was
indeed an agreeable surprise. The next morning I made all sail after a French barque,
hoping to get her longitude; but she did not
like the look of us and crowded all sail, and as

I had to shorten sail to allow the Atala to close I saw no more of her. However, I got sight of Point Hood the next day, which set my mind at rest.

From this time we had, on the whole, fine weather, and I managed to keep company by being always under easy sail, for with a foul wind I got so much to windward that the schooner took a whole day coming up, and I seriously thought of leaving her at one time, for my crew were getting sick, and three of the best were in their hammocks, leaving me only seven; but we fortunately got fair winds and ran along the land, making Cape Recif, St. Francis, Plettenberg, and all the different points as far as Agulhas, which we rounded in company, within ten miles, at night; and on the morning of the 21st of December made all sail to a strong south-easterly wind, which took us into Simon's Bay by 4 P.M.

All the way up False Bay we had studding-sails on both sides, and gradually shortened sail to topsails before rounding to, but I did not reef, and found it blowing a perfect gale in Simon's Bay. Away went the clue of my jib, and the little brig spun along throwing the spray fore and aft. However, I brought her well to windward, and thought myself all right, when the cable got a riding turn over the windlass, in consequence of which I drifted within forty yards of the beach, when, with the assistance of the boats of our ship which had just arrived, we brought up with three anchors ahead and made all snug by dark; and I had the pleasure of shaking Alexander by the hand, and found that both the Progresso and Defensivo had been condemned in the Admiralty Court. Though close to the beach blowing a gale it was the first night's rest I had for three weeks.

Young Wrey, who was with me, proved himself, during the passage, an excellent observer and navigator. On the 23rd I got to Cape Town with Lehenson to bring our vessels into court, but found that nothing could be done until after the Christmas holidays, which gave me an opportunity of spending three or four days most pleasantly with my kind friends; and having made affidavits as to the circumstances under which the vessels were taken, had them condemned and broken up; the brig measuring 235 and the Atala 152 tons.

From the day of our arrival to January 26, 1844, on which we sailed, we experienced a constant succession of south-easterly gales, which made it extremely disagreeable refitting, and knocked about the boats a great deal. In going on shore we were covered with spray, and the fine sand blowing in our wet faces and drying in with a burning sun caused a continual smart, and makes the summer at the Cape very disagreeable. I left the little black boy Jozé at Belmont, where he has every prospect of being well thought of and provided for.

We anchored at St. Augustine's Bay on February 14, and were soon surrounded by our old friends. Prince Green came on board in a tattered old dressing gown, his sable countenance radiant with smiles, and held out his hand to Caswell, who being in the heat of carrying on duty, gave him the cold shoulder; and the surprise depicted on his face was truly amusing, as he drew himself up, saying in the most confident manner, "Me, Prince

Green." On the 16th, a heavy swell setting in warned us of an approaching gale, and we got a good offing without waiting for stocks, and on the 17th and 18th washed away our head and bumpkin, and stove in several ports, the barometer falling to 29·23.

On February 24th we anchored off Quillimane, and I was sent up to the town in the barge, taking with me Norman and Lyttleton, and on landing was met by Senhor Ambrozio Terceira Mourão, who asked me if I was Senhor Barnardo, as he had been left in charge of the house during the absence of Senhor Azvedo, who desired me to make myself as much at home as if he was there himself. In the evening I called on the Governor, and found that Azvedo had given the Concorde for the service of Her Most Faithful Majesty, and that it was intended to endeavour to bring her from Macuzé to Quillimane; and in a letter to Captain Wyvill which I took down with me, the Governor requested that I might be allowed to undertake the service, which, of course was out of the question, our means of checking the slave trade being little enough without our weakening them.

I found here my old acquaintance Said Hamza, whose barque I had taken possession of at Johanna for the King. After we left the vessel was restored, and he went to Comoro and took in a cargo of bullocks for Mozambique, but was set by the current to the southward and bore up for Quillimane, where he struck on the bar and made so much water that he was obliged to run her on shore off the town, where she has become a complete wreck. In my conversation with this man I found that he was very likely to prove most useful in gaining information respecting the slave trade, and I acted accordingly. He told me that it was going on very briskly, and that a black schoooner had sailed from Macuzé full, within the last month. Senhor Moraes, Azvedo's father-in-law, had died, leaving a large property. The Brazilian agent was still residing there; and the Governor had made 60,000 dollars in fifteen months by peculation and slave fees.

I returned on the 27th, and after looking into all the rivers to the southward and northward of Quillimane, anchored off Casuauna to cut wood and to repair our damages. This

island is covered with tall straight trees of iron-
wood, and abounds in very beautiful shrubs.
On the beach are the remains of turtle which
the natives from the neighbourhood of Quizungo
come over for yearly. We found fresh water
in an old pit, about six feet from the surface;
but on digging deeper and sinking a cask
found it so brackish that it could not be used,
so that the other must have been merely rain
water. The rats are so numerous that the
men knocked them over with sticks, and
roasted them, declaring they were exactly like
chicken,—"no accounting for taste."

On the night of March 10th, about ten
o'clock, we observed a sail running down on
us, and in a few minutes hailed the Bittern,
and in the morning Captain Peel came on
board, and we afterwards stood towards the
Elephant Shoals in company, when finding
nothing, we hove to, and our friends came on
board to dinner. The Bittern had spent her
Christmas at Delagoa Bay, and had been
placed in rather an awkward position in
getting out. The sea broke heavily across the
passage, and was one sheet of foam; however

our old master Blackford, whose coolness never
forsakes him, said "You must keep her at it;
there were six fathoms when we came in, and
there must be the same now;" and through it
she went, shipping two regular green seas.
They had also been at Mozambique, where,
whilst the men were bathing, one poor fellow
lost his leg by the bite of a shark, which
literally tore the flesh off the bones. The following day we parted company, the brig
standing in for the land, and the frigate for
St. Augustine's Bay, expecting to meet again
off Quillimane on the 1st of April.

From the 12th to the 18th we experienced
very light south-easterly breezes, and found
great difficulty in getting to eastward. On the
evening of the 18th we passed close to the
Bassas da India Rocks, a most dangerous shoal
with here and there a black rock, which cannot in
the finest weather be seen more than five or six
leagues off from the masthead, and the currents
are so changeable and uncertain all round it,
that without a good commanding breeze, a ship
is likely to be drifted on it in spite of herself,
which was actually the case with the Julia,

whose dreadful loss will be related in a subsequent page. After passing this, we continued to work our way to the eastward, and at sunset on the 21st saw the land from the mast-head, and at 6 P.M. got the lat. by Canopus. Just after eight o'clock the Master came down, and said the Captain wished to stand on a little longer to make the most of it; and we were sitting, chatting as usual in the gun-room, about 10 P.M, when the well-known and dreaded feel of her keel grating along the bottom, made us all rush on deck, where we found the Captain, First Lieutenant, and Master. Having just determined to tack, and waiting only for a cast of the deep-sea lead, which had already been sent forward, two minutes more would have saved us from all the misery and dreadful scenes which I am about to detail.

At 8h. 30m., P. M., the officer of the watch ordered two leadsmen in the chains, and at nine there was no bottom with fifty-five fathoms of line, and the hand lead was kept constantly going until 9h. 50m., when the land was seen on the lee-bow, and a cast of the deep-sea

lead ordered by the Captain, while everything
was seen clear for going about, and in a few
seconds the helm would have been put down,
when she touched. Everything was immediately
thrown aback, and she moved astern, but her
keel hanging, she fell off with her head in-
shore, and became imbedded in coral-rocks,
with from two and a half to three fathoms
round her, the tide being about half-ebb. As
soon as the ship would clear it, the small
bower was let go and veered to about thirty
fathoms, to keep her from forging in-shore when
the tide rose, and the Master was sent in the
cutter to sound round her, whilst the barge and
pinnace were hoisted out, and the stream
anchor and kedge and the two stream cables
and hemp messenger got into them. In the
mean time a channel was found on the port-
bow, and the stream anchor backed by the
kedge, was laid out in that direction by Molesworth and Norman, but never hove taut, as on
further sounding there was a deeper and better
channel found astern and off-shore. Whilst
the boats were away the sails were furled, the
best bower unshackled, and the chain messenger

passed through the stern hawse hole and brought
to the main-deck capstan, which was disconnected and rigged on the main-deck. On the
return of the boats after laying out the stream,
the best bower anchor was got under the pinnace, which was fortunately fitted with trunks
and a windlass, and the two hemp sheet
cables were coiled on the thwarts of the barge,
whilst the Master laid out hawsers with
second kedge for warping them out; and about
4 A. M., the arrangements being completed, the
sheet cable was passed through the midship
cabin port, the hawse hole not being large
enough to admit the cook's leg, and the best
bower was laid on the port quarter in good
style.

At 6 A. M., the tide being at its highest, a
taut strain was hove on the sheet and she
moved astern about twenty fathoms, the small
bower being brought to the upper deck capstan,
by the top tackle pendants, for a messenger
with runners and tackles on the main-deck to
assist. We now found that the stern had got
on a patch of coral, which had close by the
side of it a three fathom channel, and Moles-

worth and the Master were sent in the barge
and pinnace to weigh the stream, and kedge
and lay them out on the starboard quarter. This
was a work of time, as the anchors had hooked
the rocks, and the tide began to fall before they
were ready; and in the interim, the small bower
was hove up, minus a stock, and the men were
allowed a short time to splice the main brace
and get their breakfasts.

At 8 A.M., we commenced heaving on both
capstans, the stream cable being led through the
starboard after-quarter deck port. But the tide
had receded too much ; and finding she did not
start, the top-gallant masts were got on deck,
and the people sent down for three hours' rest
just as she went over on her bilge, the water
being up to the sills of the main-deck ports on
the starboard side. Fortunately the weather was
calm and fine, for had even a moderate swell
set in, she must have been bilged; as it was,
she bumped most uncomfortably and made the
masts and yards rattle and tremble as if they
were coming down about our heads.

At low water the reefs were dry all round
us, one sheet of copper being in the water at

one side, and the muzzles of the guns all but
touching the water on the other, and one could
as easily walk on the outside of the ship as
the deck. The hatches were battened down and
all hands seated themselves on the main-deck,
either breakfasting or snatching a few minutes'
rest. In the morning we had observed two or
three canoes approaching to within about half
a mile of the ship, and then make for the
shore, and during the forenoon from twenty to
thirty came off in line, and dodged about
under the bows, conversing with the boat-
keepers in broken English, as is customary with
the natives of St. Augustine's Bay; and having
been in the habit of treating them with confidence, no one had any doubt of their friendly
intentions. In one canoe was an old man with
a bald head and grey beard, who appeared to
take the lead, being paddled by two men and
not working himself. On our commencing
work again, they all dispersed, some going on
shore, others to the reefs, as if for shells, and
it is reported that one of them said, "To-
morrow King Baba come take the ship: he
give the Captain plenty sheep, and plenty

bullock, and make him stop; but he want the ship." This was thought nothing of, and about half-past ten, the Captain called the First Lieutenant, Master, and myself, to consult as to what was most expedient to be done, and we all agreed that she ought to he lightened to ensure her getting off the following tide, and about noon we hoisted out the small boats; the Master went to buoy the passage, and all hands commenced constructing a raft with the spare spars and casks to hold the guns.

At 3 P. M., we finished and hoisted it out, and got two quarter-deck guns on it, when the water having risen, she began to right, and the capstans were manned, and she started some distance; but at 5 P. M., finding her still hard aground, the order was given to throw the foremost main-deck guns overboard, and the two 8-inch, and one forecastle gun went, and two more quarter-deck guns were got on the raft, when we again tried her and succeeded in heaving her into five fathoms water, but in the midst of coral patches. The chain gauger just came into the stern port and was secured, and the small bower cable brought along out-

side and shackled to it, ready to heave her
head round in the morning. The guns and the
boats were hoisted in, the raft dismantled, and
at midnight the men were sent to rest for four
hours, thoroughly fagged out ; but throughout
the whole, I never heard a murmur or complaint, and never feared the result.

From 12 to 4, the ship bumped heavily,
and ground along the rocks, and at 1, the
stream cable parted, having been chafed
through; and nothing could exceed our anxiety
during the night, as she was riding by twelve
fathoms of chain only, by the stern, and had
we drove, our position would have been worse
than ever. At 4, the hands were turned up
and the top-gallant mast fidded, and top-
gallant yards crossed, and the Master took the
barge, and Molesworth the pinnace, to endeavour to get the stream and kedge anchors; but
the boats being wanted on board, they were
recalled, and at 6, the sheet cable was slipt
from the stern port, and her head hove to
seaward by the small bower cable, and all
plain sail made to a light land breeze. When
the anchor was weighed she went some distance,

and then hung on a coral patch, when a kedge was laid out with a hawser right ahead, which took us into deep water, and finding her running over it faster than we could haul in, Molesworth was called in the pinnace to take in the bight of the hawser, which we cut, and to remain to weigh the anchor.

We had observed, all the morning, the canoes coming off as before towards the ship, and as they would necessarily pass close to the pinnace, the Captain ordered a look-out to be kept on them; and we were about 400 yards from the boat when the wind fell so light that it required the nicest attention to keep our head the right way; and at 7h. 30m. the sea breeze took us aback, and the ship wore round with her head in shore, and at the same time, Molesworth was observed making a signal for assistance. The pinnace-men were splashing their oars, and apparently cutting the hawser, and the boat then came towards us, pulled only by four oars, whilst the canoes made sail and paddled with all their might towards the shore.

The galley and barge went immediately to

their assistance, and the ship was hove-to, and every preparation was made in case of accidents, and a fearful sight soon met our eyes. The pinnace had been attacked by the natives, two of the crew killed, Lieutenant Molesworth, and five men, mortally wounded, and three severely and dangerously wounded;—three only escaping out of fourteen.

Poor Molesworth was wounded in the nose and bowels, and on my jumping into the boat, he exclaimed, with a look of despair, "My God, Barnard, I am wounded in the bowels." I immediately lifted him into a cot which had been lowered by a whip from the main yard, and remained in the boat until all the wounded were hoisted in. The groans of the poor sufferers were heartrending, and their bodies were covered with ghastly wounds: it was a truly pitiable sight, and in lifting them my hand went frequently into a deep hole, the spears having passed quite through them. At first some hopes were entertained of poor Molesworth's recovery, but on Sunday, March 24, such unfavourable symptoms showed themselves, that it was thought right to advise him

G 3

to settle his affairs.   He bore the shock like a strong-minded man, made his will, and thought of everything the most minute.   That evening he received the sacrament, and calmly took leave of all his messmates, appearing perfectly resigned.   In the night he grew uneasy and restless, and at half-past ten on Monday he departed this life, his lips having moved, as if in prayer, not long before, and in the evening he was followed to his watery grave by all his shipmates, universally regretted, and admired for his noble and manly conduct.

The cause of this murderous attack appears to have been as follows :—On the canoes approaching the pinnace, poor Molesworth commenced talking to them, as to the natives at St. Augustine's Bay, asking if they had any harp shells, on which they approached the boat closer, and two of them got into her unarmed as if for barter, and seized the iron bars belonging to the windlass.   On this, they were ordered out, and force used to eject them, Molesworth jumping forward to enforce their going, on which a spear was thrown which wounded him in the nose, and seemed to be the signal for a general attack; the old bald-headed man with a grey beard, twirling a spear round his head, and then giving weapons to those around him. Poor Jacobs, the bowman, who hauled me into the boat when I was upset at Quillimane, received a spear in the shoulder which knocked him overboard, and on rising to the surface his brains were knocked out, and nothing saved the whole from being massacred, but the ship's being providentially taken aback, and appearing to the savages to be coming towards them. The whole was the work of two minutes, or even less, and although our poor fellows made a desperate resistance, unarmed and lumbered up as they were, the sharp spears hurled with tremendous force soon laid them low.

The opinions as to the intentions of the natives when coming off are various: our first impression was that they had come to attack the ship, if they found us off our guard, and that savage disappointment at not finding us a wreck, had roused their evil passions. The more common opinion, however, is that they had no end in view, but mere curiosity;

but their savage nature is such, that it is always a word and a blow with them, and that at the least provocation they instinctively use their arms. Would that all these suppositions could change the results, and restore the fine fellows who fell.

After the canoes had fled, there was no possibility of reaching them, as they escaped over the reefs on which our boats could not float, and even if our guns could have sunk a few of them, the dreadful state of the wounded rendered it impossible to fire; and they are such a wandering race that they have no fixed village or habitations, generally ranging up and down the coast, and living in their canoes.

On March 25th, we anchored in St. Augustine's Bay, and remained five days watering and getting to rights. The channel at the entrance of the river was much altered, and enabled us to water much quicker. Many of my old friends came to see me, and express their horror at the treachery of their countrymen; but I would not trust myself alone with them without being well armed, for I fancy they all go occasionally on predatory excursions along the coast. Some of the natives offered me slaves for sale, and I pretended to want them, that I might find out if any great number could be obtained, but found that there were only a few, principally young girls, stolen or taken in fight from the Ovas. The price of them was twenty dollars, or a keg of powder, but without an agent to collect them, I do not imagine any vessel could get a cargo.

CHAPTER V.

LUDICROUS ACCIDENT.—AZVEDO'S HOSPITALITY.—SLAVES BURNT ALIVE.—THE BLACK SCHOONER.—MORGADO'S GRAND DINNER.—DR. PETERS.—THE COLONOS.—WILLING SLAVES.—INVITATION TO A BALL.—A SAIL AHEAD.—BOARD A SLAVER.—MUTINY AND MURDER.—MR. HILL'S FIFTY DAYS ON BOARD A SLAVER.—WRECK OF THE JULIA.—THE DON PEDRO.—THE MINERVA.—THE PINNACE FOUND.—ATTEMPT TO HEAVE UP THE GUNS.—MURDERER'S REEFS.—ANCHOR IN SIMON'S BAY.

ON the morning of April 14th, we arrived in Simon's Bay, but found that the Admiral had not arrived from the West Coast, and I rode up the same afternoon for our letters, and had the pleasure of seeing my friends who were of course much shocked at my melancholy tale; and at the request of Captain Broke, I waited upon the Governor Sir Peregrine Maitland, to give him a correct version of our misfortune, and on returning to Simon's Bay, found that we were ready for sea in a week, so that I was obliged to return to Cape Town for the purpose of laying in stock, and had a most amusing adventure on the road.

The driver of the mail cart dropped the letter-bag on the road, and Lieutenant Kane took the reins whilst he rode back to look for it, and we had not gone far, before the horses shyed at a cart of rushes which was upset in the road, run up a bank and turned us over. Kane got jammed and could not move, a lady and her maid who were inside, were more frightened than hurt, and I pulled them out from amongst a heap of boxes, and it all ended in laughter; and the coachman having come up in the meantime, we soon righted the cart without any damage. That evening I went to the race ball, and on the 20th, Captain Broke kindly drove me down in his tandem. The next morning we sailed, but had scarcely rounded Noah's Ark, when we saw the Winchester, and in the evening anchored in company, and I had the happiness of hearing that my brother was on board, and the following day he joined the Cleopatra. The Winchester during her cruise had succeeded in destroying a slaver, and various changes and promotions took place, in consequence of the death of Captain Farr, of the Conway, and our poor messmate, Molesworth. On the 23rd, we again sailed, taking with us an old harbour-boat to assist in raising the guns we had left on the coast of Madagascar.

On May 12th, we anchored off Quillimane, and the next morning I left for Quillimane, accompanied by Mr. Steel, our chaplain, and my brother, and after anchoring outside the bar until the flood made, we had a most delightful sail up the river, for all was new to my companions, and they had some famous shots at the hippopotami, one of which got out of the water and ran into the jungle not forty yards from the boat. On arriving at the town we were received by Senhor Azvedo, with his usual hospitality, and in the evening made a short excursion in machilas, excepting Jack, who preferred a mule, which was a source of great amusement to us; for the sight of anything in the shape of a horse is so rare here, that the Blacks fly from it in every direction, as if it was some wild beast, and the little boys run behind at a respectable distance, whooping and making a noise.

I seized one of them and put him up behind Jack before he was aware of it, and giving the brute a crack sent him off full gallop. The little fellow hung on like grim death, and they rolled about like a ship in a calm. In the evening I learnt that about a week before our arrival, a large barque had embarked from 700 to 800 slaves at Ouilinda, the river to the southward of Quillimane, and I have since found out, that this was the same Julia which Trou, the captain of the Gentil, had detained in May last, and that the slaves actually went from the town of Quillimane in launches. Three or four days after our last visit, 300 slaves had been burnt alive in a baracoon some distance to the northward, where they had been sent ready for embarkation, one of them slipping his iron collar during the night, and setting fire to the building.

Upwards of 2,000 slaves were ready in the neighbourhood of the town for embarkation, purchased with merchandize, brought out by American vessels, and slave-vessels were ex-

pected from Rio daily, so that my arrival at
Quillimane put those who had so much at
stake in a great ferment, and I witnessed long
and angry discussions amongst them as they
came in and out of Azvedo's house. A brig,
said to be under Sardinian colours, had attempted to land her captain at Luabo, where
they say there is a flag-staff, but he with
three of his boat's crew was drowned in crossing the bar, one man only reaching the
shore, and no more has been heard of her.

The black schooner belonging to Senhor
Isidore, which had embarked 400 slaves at
Macuze, put back after having lost one-half of
her human cargo, and relanded the wretched
remnant half dead.

Paulo Roderigue who commanded the Defensivo, had written to his friends at Quillimane blaming them for giving me his name,
and accusing Azvedo as being the cause of his
losing his vessel, and the Governor had received letters from Lisbon, informing him that
Lord Aberdeen had written to the Portuguese
Ministry, saying that he was not to be trusted
as he was open to bribery. His friends also

advised him to be on his guard against the former collector of customs, Senhor Azvedo, who was in the habit of giving information to the English. Said Hamza corroborated most of the above information, not knowing that I had heard anything from other quarters, and declared that he was narrowly watched whilst the English flag was flying in the river. Indeed the trade seems to be on the increase, and all servants who speak English or are likely to converse with the boat's crew, are sent into the interior..

It is said that a person who deals largely in human flesh at Quillimane, is about to endeavour to establish a place for embarking slaves near Sofala, but this cannot be managed for some time, as the Governor of that place must first be bought over. Nothing can exceed the civility and hospitality of the inhabitants of Quillimane. Their houses are always open to the English, and on our arrival Senhor Morgado invited us to a supper the next evening; but having a spare day, we took advantage of permission from the Governor to ascend farther up the river, and we got

Azvedo to accompany us, and had a most delightful sail for about fifteen miles.

The appearance of the banks improves greatly after passing Quillimane: the mangrove-trees with their dense foliage reach to the very water, and look as beautifully green and fresh as they are deadly and sickly: no ray of the sun can penetrate them from one year's end to the other, and the thick slimy mud produces the fatal miasma, myriads of musquitoes, and a kind of large fly which darts its lance into the flesh and draws blood immediately. Here and there a break in the jungle shews the track of hippopotami, which in herds of eight or ten quite line the banks, and with flock after flock of pelicans, flamingoes, wild-ducks, and all kinds of sea fowl, keep the attention amply engaged, and afford excellent marks for expending powder and shot on.

The following day we were invited to a grand dinner by Senhor Morgado, and at about 3 P.M. sat down to a table groaning under the good things of this world. Mountains of rice, roast pig, ducks, fowls, herons, mutton, beef, venison, raised pies, calavances, spinach and eggs, were all crowded together, and twelve sat down to a dinner enough for a hundred; and I was not a little surprised to see men, apparently suffering from a horrid fever, playing as good a stick as those in rude health. A short life and a merry one seems to be their creed, and few of them ever return to their own country. However, on this occasion, we followed their example, and did ample justice to the hospitality of our host.

After dinner sundry complimentary toasts were drunk, and as I was considered the principal guest, the health of Senhor Barnardo and family was reserved for the last, according to the Portuguese custom. I had to return thanks, and begged, on the present occasion, to make an exception to the general rule, and drink the "Health and hospitality of Senhor Morgado," which was drunk with "broas," and each smashed his glass, excepting ourselves, who thought it rather an equivocal way of showing our gratitude. After much difficulty I managed to get away, all hands accompanying me to the beach, and expressing great regret that I was determined

to go. The wind was so light, that I did not
get above half way down the river, and we all
spent a most miserable night in the boats,
crowded up with ducks and fowls, and all
kinds of stock, and the next day, after much
difficulty, we got on board about 2 P.M., not
at all the better for having rolled about in a
heavy swell in the Well after our feasting.

On May 22nd, we observed a vessel at
anchor, and made all sail towards her, and
soon perceived that she was at anchor in the
Well, and I was forthwith despatched in the
barge to find out all about her, and she
proved to be the Amizade from Mozambique
with passengers, amongst whom was my old
friend Dr. Peters, on his way to Senna and
Tete, and we were mutually delighted at
meeting so unexpectedly. On the 25th he
accompanied me down the river, intending to
pay Captain Wyvill a visit, but after remaining at the Point all night, we found the bar
too rough to attempt crossing; so leaving the
barge in charge of my brother, I took Peters
to the town in the dingy, and returned to the
Point in the night, ready to take advantage of

the land breeze in the morning, which enabled
me to get outside; but it was raining so hard,
that they did not perceive me from the ship
until within a mile of her.

About Quillimane and Luabo, and indeed
in all the Portuguese possessions on the coast,
are numbers of Colonos, or free blacks, who
hire themselves out as wood-cutters, machila-
bearers, or labourers, and such is the degraded
state of society that these men are taunted by
the slaves as having no white man to look after
them, and see them righted when oppressed.
They are kept in subjection by a very severe
and separate code of laws, and if they break
or injure anything which they cannot pay for
they become slaves. After the death of Moraes,
Azvedo's father-in-law, who was a very severe
master, no less than eighty slaves, who had
deserted and escaped into the interior, returned
to the estate and resumed their work, prefer-
ring slavery to the iron rule of the chiefs of
their own colour: others come frequently to
sell themselves, and to buy them is the greatest
boon a good master can bestow, and their price
is from three to five pieces of clouty or dungaree.

Azvedo relates an anecdote of a man who
day after day had been importuning him to
take him as a slave, and, when he found that he
could not get rid of his freedom by fair means,
he watched the opportunity whilst Azvedo's
little boy was walking in the garden with his
nurse and tore the child's frock, which created
a great hubbub and noise, and the father running out found his son dreadfully frightened
and the black rolling in the dirt according to
the custom of his country. Embracing his
feet he cried out, that as he had refused to
buy him, he had torn his child's frock, and
having nothing to pay for it he was his slave
by the law of the country; so seeing he was so
determined he gave him his clouty, and he has
worked away steadily ever since.

Amongst the passengers in the brig was a
man named Villa Real, who had originally got
a passage to Quillimane at the Government
expense, for (as he himself describes it) merely
giving a man a friendly punch in the stomach
when he had unfortunately, by pure accident,
a small knife in his hand. He has now amassed
a small fortune by slave-dealing, like many

others here, and such are the kind of people one meets, and many a murderer receives a stranger with a polite bow and shake of the hand.

It was supposed that the death of Romās and Moraes, the two capitalists of Quillimane, and the life and soul of the slave trade, would reduce this horrid traffic as there are no others who could run so great a risk; but I see no reason to suppose that it is at all decreasing, nor will it, until the governors and officers of the customs have a sufficient salary to induce them to act honestly.

On June 12th Alexander started in charge of the pinnace for Quillimane, accompanied by Parker, O'Hagan, and Jago, but before reaching the bar a sail hove in sight and they boarded her. We anchored, and before daylight I started in the cutter and ran down to the stranger, whom I found anchored on the bar with the pinnace astern, both of them rolling most awfully; and a miserable night they must have had of it. The brig was the Domingo Cardoza, alias Biscoito, from Mozambique, and never did I see such an old clum-

H

bungy; so leaky that the pumps were constantly going. Not a rope was in her that was
not fagged out or knotted in several places;
her sails were so rotten and full of holes that
they were afraid to set them; and she was
riding in a heavy sea with a more than
half-worn coù cable. How these fellows
escape I know not! She was commanded
by the Commissaire of the Gentil, and I
learnt from him that the Governor-General
was to leave Mozambique for Lorenzo Macques
on the 15th, on reporting which to the Captain
he recalled the pinnace and started for Mozambique, where we arrived on the 19th, and
found that the General was expected on the
1st of August, having left on the 9th instant.

One evening a grand ball was given by Captain Chavres and Senhor Delphin Oliveria, it
being the first anniversary of their wedding-day.
Captain Wyvill's invitation amused us much,
it commenced thus: "Monsieur, j'ai l'honneur
vous inviter prendre une tasse du thé chez moi,
avec votre *corporation*, &c." Every body went
but the Captain and myself, and returned on
board from a very tame affair, tired and dis-

satisfied, and we sailed in the morning crowded up with bullocks and all kinds of stock.

On the 1st July, being off Quillimane, we espied and made all sail towards a stranger, which proved to be a Portuguese brig. I boarded her in the gig and found her to be the Esperanza from Lisbon and Rio, bound to Quillimane, Mozambique, and Bombay. I examined her papers and hold, and seeing nothing suspicious I gave them ample directions for crossing the bar and returned on board. I learnt from her that she had been boarded by the Bittern a few days before, which had driven on shore and burnt a brigantine, and had gone to the northward with a Brazilian vessel, supposed to be a prize.

After this we stood to the southward, and on the evening of the 3rd, being under all sail returning to the northward, observed a sail ahead; but the wind being light, and having no chance of coming up with her that night, we shortened sail to the topsails, trusting that she might not see us, and soon after anchored in a calm. At four the next morning a breeze enabled us to make all sail, and at daylight

we observed our friend at anchor off Quillimane, and were soon rejoiced to see him make
sail away from us, and the wind falling light I
was sent away in the galley to cut him off,
and after a long and exciting chase boarded a
fine brig fully equipped for the slave trade,
about half a mile from the shore, and I very
soon had her head towards the ship under all
sail. All her crew had deserted but five, and
she had no papers nor colours, and was loaded
with water, farinha, rice, and beans. Caswell
and the Master came on board to survey her,
and the prisoners were removed to the ship
who stood on in company with us, and in the
evening I was left in charge to take her to the
anchorage off Quillimane. I found a capital
chronometer, quadrant, spy-glass, and charts;
and in the morning saw the ship standing
towards me under all sail; but on a squall's
clearing up, which had concealed her from me,
I observed that she had hauled her wind and
soon had the satisfaction of seeing her heave
to with a large barque in company, and I soon
after anchored in company with them off
Quillimane; but it was blowing too fresh to
communicate.

In the lining of the pilot's hat I found a paper, signed by the brig's crew, and it appeared her name was the Zäcette de Marco, and that her crew had mutinied off Delagoa Bay and put the captain on shore, obliging the pilot to take her to Quillimane against his will. (I found out afterwards that they had murdered the captain and thrown him overboard.) Amongst his papers I found numbers of prints of our Saviour, the Virgin Mary, and a host of saints;—the following was underneath one of them:—

"N. S. Da Socorro

"O Exm. Snr. Bispo. concede 40 dias de indulgce as todas as pessoas qt. diante desta imagem rezavera hum P N e che M N S."

"Our Lady of Succour.

"His Excellency the Bishop concedes 40 days' indulgence to all persons who before this image shall recite one Pater Noster," &c.

On the sixth we communicated with the ship, and I found that the barque was a prize named the Izabel fitted as a slaver, and I gave up charge of the brig to Lieutenant Caswell, who was ordered to remain off Quillimane to watch that river, whilst we ran the coast up and down for a fortnight.

On July 7th, Alexander sailed for the Cape, taking half the prisoners and two invalids, and we sailed on a cruize, leaving the brig alone in her glory, rolling most awfully; and, after cruizing about the mouths of the Zambezi, returned to her on the 12th, when Caswell came on board and told us that the Sappho had arrived the day before, with our late chaplain, the Reverend P. G. Hill, and orders from the Admiralty to inquire into certain statements of his in a pamphlet entitled "Fifty Days on Board a Slaver;" and as she had gone to the northward we stood on in that direction, and the next day fell in with her. Captain Hope came on board, bringing with him many welcome letters from home, which were the more acceptable from being unexpected.

We found, from the nature of the inquiry ordered to be instituted, that it was necessary to go to the Cape to meet Alexander, whose character, as well as those of more than one officer, seemed to be indirectly attacked in this very imperfect account of the capture and subsequent history of the Progresso, which we got a copy of. In the first place, it would strike one that the order to send the slaves below the first night was unnecessary, whereas it saved many from being washed overboard. In the next place, the fifty deaths would appear to have been caused by suffocation after the order was given, whereas a dozen, if not more, dead bodies were seen some time before by the men who went down for water, and more than half the number were in a state of stupid intoxication. The next thing that struck us was the mention of Azvedo's name, as one at variance with the Governor, and as having given information. This we could not but consider as a breach of trust, as all the official letters had been expressly worded to prevent our informants' names from being brought before any authorities in whose power it might be to injure them. Consequently, I was sent to Quillimane to inform Azvedo that his name had been mentioned, and to put him on his guard, as well as to express Captain Wyvill's regret that it had happened.

On the 14th of July, I left in the barge
with Parker and O'Hagan, and after a delightful sail of three hours reached the town. I
found Azvedo at home, and we were received
with his usual hearty welcome; and on inquir-
ing for my friend Dr. Peters, I learnt that he
was in the next room, slowly recovering from
a dangerous fever; and there I found him,
poor fellow! propped up with pillows and
cushions, looking the mere shadow of what
he had been, surrounded by the Governor and
principal people of Quillimane, most of whose
lives he had probably saved; and their attention to him, and anxiety for his recovery,
seemed to know no bounds. He had been
some distance up the river, having started
with a fever on him, which he had slighted
and treated merely as a cold; but it increased
so rapidly that he was in a very reduced state
when they got him back to Quillimane, where
he met with every kindness and attention from
his old patients. We immediately saw that
his only hope of recovery was from a change
of climate, and insisted on his accompanying
us to the Cape; and, after a great deal of

persuasion from Dr. O'Hagan and myself, he was at last convinced that it was his only chance, and I promised to remain a day for him to arrange his affairs. In the evening we had a large concourse of visitors, and amongst them the Captain and passengers of the brig Esperanza, which I had boarded off the bar. I had a long conversation with the former on the slave trade, which he spoke of as a species of gambling, carried on only by persons of considerable property. For instance, a man with "400 contos of reis will risk 50 contos in the slave trade. If he succeeds, he doubles his fortune; if he loses, he has enough left. I sent letters viâ Bombay by this brig, and as they arrived safely in England, it did away with all suspicion of her being engaged in the slave trade.

I must now add another page to the dreadful horrors of slavery. The bark Julia, which I have twice mentioned before, after sailing with 700 slaves, was eight days afterwards wrecked on the Bassas da India Rocks, when every soul perished except the Captain and three of the crew, who escaped to the Macuzé in a small gig. The current had drifted them close to the breakers before they knew their danger, and they had barely time to get out of her before she opened and went down.

Thus, in the short space of six months, I have detailed the untimely end of 1,200 Negroes, by fire*, disease†, and wreck‡; and the suffering they must have endured whilst being driven from the interior must have thinned considerably the original number; for frequently have I seen them, soon after their arrival at Quillimane, mere skeletons, with death depicted in their countenances.

I saw the schooner on the beach: she was not coppered, and about ninety tons burden; and on board this were 400 human beings crammed for a passage across the Atlantic.

It was said that Paulo Roderique, the Captain of the Defensivo, was at Delagoa Bay or Inhambau with a large brig, endeavouring to get a cargo of slaves; and I afterwards learnt from the boatswain of our prize, the Isabel, that the name of the brig was the

* 300 burnt in a baracoon.
† 200 in Black schooner.   ‡ 700 in Julia.

Lagunence, and that she was at Inhambau; and this information proved quite correct, as will be seen in the sequel.

On the 16th I roused up the whole house at daybreak, being exceedingly anxious to get over the bar, so as not to have Dr. Peters in the boat all night. However, I could not get away under an hour, and lost the land-breeze before I was half way down the river; and the sea-breeze setting in strong, I became very anxious, particularly when I found, on closing the bar, that it was breaking heavily across, which obliged me to anchor in a heavy swell for four hours, which tried my poor patience very severely; but the breakers subsiding with the flood tide, I cracked on a heavy press of sail, and got on board by eight o'clock; and Captain Wyvill had his side-cabin prepared for Dr. Peters, who was much exhausted. Never did I feel greater satisfaction than when I saw him in a comfortable cot, and reflected that I had perhaps been an instrument in the hands of Providence for the preservation of a valuable life.

The Commanders of the Sappho and Bittern

were on board when I arrived, and I learnt
that the latter had been to Mokamba Bay
with a brig under Brazilian colours, which she
had detained off Quillimane, after driving a
brigantine on shore.   Her name was the Don
Pedro; and, after much difficulty, she was
found to be engaged in the slave trade by the
Mixed Commission at Sierra Leone—the man
who was acting as steward proving to be the
surgeon, having a considerable share in the
voyage.   The name of the brigantine I found
to be the Feliz.

On the 17th, Caswell sailed in our prize
brig for the coast of Madagascar, where we
had left our guns; and on the 18th we
weighed in company with the two brigs,
and parted—the Bittern standing to northward, the Sappho for the land, and the Cleopatra for the Murderer's Reefs.   On the 21st,
I boarded the Minerva, an American whaler,
who "guessed" he had seen a suspicious-looking
barque off Luabo, under French colours, the
day before we captured the Isabel, which
proved to be one and the same vessel.   On
the 29th we anchored in seventeen fathoms,

on the coast of Madagascar, about three miles
from the land, in lat. 22° 30′ South, and, as it
subsequently proved, about four or five miles
to the northward of the reef where we had
grounded and thrown our guns overboard;
and at daylight on the following morning the
boats were sent, manned and armed, in charge
of Lieutenant Norman, in search of the spot;
but on that and the following evening the
boats returned after a fruitless search.

On the 1st of August the boats left as before,
and the carpenters were set to work to make
two frames for glasses to examine the bottom;
and the Captain went in the galley to try to
catch a black fellow to shew us where the guns
were, and chased a canoe which made for the
shore, and, on landing, it required considerable coaxing and amicable signs to induce the
savages to approach, and they then could not
make themselves understood, although evidently well aware of the late treacherous
attack of their countrymen. In the meantime a small boat was sent with glasses, and
no sooner was one of them placed in the
water, than the pinnace was found to be an-

chored over the lost cable, which was a source
of great satisfaction to us, as we knew that
the guns could not be far off, and a boat was
left there all night.   In the morning all the
boats commenced searching for the guns with
three glasses, which, from their great simplicity
and usefulness, should be made in every ship.
This is done by constructing a frame, the bottom
of which is a square of glass, and on the top,
which is rather tapered, is a cover with a round
hole of about three inches in diameter; and
with this the small objects at the bottom may
be discovered.   About 7 A.M. Parker espied
bits of old nippers, &c., and soon after one of
the eight-inch guns, which we immediately
buoyed ; and the barge and pinnace were
lashed together with strong oak planks, and
shears were erected, plumbing the centre of
the opening between them, and with the
assistance of three men, who were fortunately good divers, Norman succeeded in
getting it into the pinnace, and bringing it
on board.

On the following day we made an attempt
to reach the other guns, but a heavy ground-

swell was setting in, and the whole line of coast was one complete sheet of foam, with evident symptoms of an approaching gale; consequently we got the boats in and prepared for sea. On Sunday and Monday the swell increased, and we were rolling the main deck guns under, the wind being nearly along shore; and in the evening of the latter day it so increased that the Captain deemed it prudent to weigh, which we did in good style, working the capstans separately with two messengers.

On Tuesday, August 8th, after being nearly becalmed all night, the boats were despatched at daylight, in my charge—the master preceding me in the galley; and, after a pull and sail of thirty miles, we found the cask which had been left as a buoy over the stream anchor, and soon had our boats moored over the eight-inch gun, with the shears rigged, and, after three narrow escapes of losing it by the slipping of the strops, &c., I had the satisfaction of lodging it safely in the bottom of the pinnace. We then took half an hour to dinner, and got over the thirty-two pounder, which gave me much anxiety and trouble, as we could just see the neck-ring sticking out of the coral, the rest of the gun being completely buried.

I was on the point of giving it up for the night, the sun being just on the horizon. I had sent a cutter to the ship for the rain-awnings and the lump with the anchor and chain, when I offered, as a forlorn hope, five dollars' reward to any man who would dive and reeve a piece of three-yarn nettle-stuff through a small hole which they had dug with a marlinespike. A young fellow named Kirkaldie dived, and succeeded. I married the end to a length of two-inch, coaxed it through the neck-ring, and up came the gun with a good hearty song from our lads, who were so pleased that they disdained the slow process of heaving it up with the windlass. At 7 h. 30 m. we got alongside, and soon saw our barkers in their old places, after a day's work that every one of us will long remember. The ship had stood in during the day, and anchored, and we remained until the following morning, hoping that Caswell would make his appear-

ance in our prize, for which we began to feel
some little anxiety.

During our stay here we had seen a few
canoes in shore, but they appeared anxious to
avoid any communication with us. At low
water the reefs are quite dry, and form a
lagoon, about a mile or a mile and a-half
wide, which seems to extend all along the
coast, rendering it safe for the natives to
work up and down in their smallest canoes
to gather l'oseille, a kind of moss, which
produces a beautiful scarlet dye, and is an
article of great trade between Tallear and St.
Augustine's Bay and the Mauritius.

On Friday, August 9th, we sailed from
Murderer's reefs with lighter hearts and more
pleasing anticipations than when, four months
before, we were surrounded by our dead and
dying shipmates, with a part of our armament
destroyed, and great doubt as to the amount
of injury sustained by the ship. On the fol-
day we anchored in St. Augustine's Bay, and
remained three days to water and get fresh
provisions. Prince Willie pretended to be
very indignant at the treacherous attack of

King Baba, and told some of the officers
that he had three bullocks and two female
slaves, which he had taken from the enemy,
and intended them for Captain Wyvill.

On the 24th of August, after a famous passage, we anchored in Simon's Bay, and found
there the Cornwallis, Winchester, Isis, Conway,
and Thunderbolt, and in a few days we heard
that our prize barque, the Isabel, had been
wrecked in Algoa Bay, and on September
13th Alexander and his crew joined, having
lost their kits. Several men were severely
bruised, but fortunately no lives were lost.
As soon as the vessel struck, her keel remained
fixed, and her whole upper works parted and
drove on the beach. She was old and rotten,
and built with spike nails instead of bolts.

On the 11th the Bittern arrived, and gave us
the welcome intelligence of the safety of our
prize brig, which had left St. Augustine's Bay
before them, and she arrived safely on the
16th. Both vessels were condemned in the
Admiralty Court, the brig having no papers,
and those of the barque being false.

CHAPTER VI.

LARGE EXPORT OF SLAVES.—NATIVES OF THE ZOOLU
COUNTRY.—IMMINENT DANGER OF A PORTUGUESE
BRIG.—HIPPOPOTAMUS POINT.—AN OLD FRIEND.—
BOARD THE JUAVO ADELAIDE.—INTERVIEW AND
DINNER WITH THE GOVERNOR OF MAJUNGA.—ALEX-
ANDER'S WHISKERS.—THE GOVERNOR'S GUARD.—HIS
DRESS.—PUNISHMENT OF A CULPRIT.—THE QUEEN OF
MAJUNGA.—RELIGION OF THE NATIVES.—SUSPICIOUS
CRUIZER.—HORSA HORSA.—INTERVIEW WITH THE
NEW GOVERNOR OF QUILLIMANE.—CAPTURE OF A
SLAVE BRIG.

ON the 20th of October, we anchored
off Quillimane, and on the 21st, Parker
and myself, took the boats up to the town,
where we arrived about 11. A. M., and the
house of our kind friend, Azvedo, was soon
crowded with all the inhabitants to congratulate
Dr. Peters on his recovery and improved appearance. On our way up the river I boarded
the American brigantine, Porpoise, and the
boat's crew recognized two of the men who
had belonged to our prize, the Defensivo: she
had also as passengers, bound to Rio, Paulo
Roderique, the captain of the said Defensivo,

and Tavaces a slave-agent, to whom our prize, the Isabel, had been consigned. I learnt that since our departure in July, Paulo Roderique had been very active in shipping slaves at Inhambau, and Delagoa Bay, having succeeded in getting off two vessels with 500 and 600 from the former place, and one with 400 from the latter. The first two of the above mentioned, are the Lagunence, reported by the boatswain of the Isabel as being on the coast, and the Kentucky, the same brig that was off the town of Quillimane with the Anna, both under American colours. The latter we captured off Luabo, fully equipped for the slave trade.

Off the town I found a rakish-looking Portuguese brig, called the Juavo Adelaide, late the Auriente, and before that the American clipper, Columbia. Her captain requested me to visit her, and tell him if there was anything on board likely to get him into a scrape. I found that she was in ballast, and fitted for passengers, amongst whom were all the slave agents but one, who merely remains to collect some money, and has written to his em-

ployers to say, that it is impossible to carry
on the trade, whilst the coast is so well guarded.
At a subsequent period, I learnt that this brig
had been purchased at Angola, by a Major
Campos, who came to Quillimane for the
ostensible purpose of agriculture, but he soon
died of fever in a hut, after purchasing a number of slaves for exportation; and no doubt
this very brig would have made a run, had we
not been on the coast.

The whole of the interior was overrun by a
tribe from the Zoulu country, in the neighbourhood of Delagoa Bay, called by the different
names of Vatuas, Landins, or Mapazetas: they
are represented as being exceedingly cruel, destroying every thing in their way, and giving
no quarter to man, woman, or child; still their
object does not appear the forming any new
settlement, and they remain quiet for three or
four years, and then destroy the whole face of
the country with fire and arrows.   Their
present irruptions seem to have been caused by
the Boers from Natal having taken possession
of their land, and driven them amongst the
tribes in the neighbourhood of the Portuguese

possessions, which can hardly be called safe from their ravages. Even a few miles from the forts (*so called*), the soldiers in these are for the most part composed of tribes who consider the Landins invulnerable, and never attempt to stand before them, and the very few Europeans amongst them are convicts from Lisbon, worn out by disease and debased by crime.

I took the water-casks up with me, but finding the water very bad at the town, I sent the boats up a branch of the river, named the Licuara ; but they could not ascend far enough in one day, and returned unsuccessful ; so I filled up with the best I could get, and made several attempts to get out to the ship, but found the bar impassable, and on the 25th I went on board the Portuguese brig, which had dropped down the river and was getting under weigh with a light wind, a heavy swell, and a strong ebb tide. I offered my assistance which was declined, and ten minutes afterwards, she was in one of the most awful predicaments a ship ever escaped from. The current had set her into the midst of the breakers, one of which struck her on her broadside, making a clean breach over her, as high as the tops. Every thing was in the greatest confusion on board, sails flying in all directions, some up, others half up or down, and to complete the folly of the thing, down went the anchor, which brought her head on to the current, and stern to the breakers, one of which pooped her, unshipped and broke her rudder, and started the whole of the stern frame. They then managed to weigh, and drifted into deep water, where they anchored.

All this occurred in less time than I have been writing it, and while I was pulling round the breakers as hard as I could, with the hope of saving some of their lives, I felt convinced that she must have gone to pieces. When I got on her deck they had not recovered from their fright, and all looked as pale as ghosts, excepting the Captain, who seemed to be the only man on board with his wits about him, and he told me that his men were all petrified, and had dropped on their knees to pray the moment the brig struck. The pilot, through whose ignorance the disaster had occurred, came up to me in the most polite way, and

offered to take my boat to the ship, by a *very
safe passage.* Nice disinterested young man.
He had that morning told me that it was not
safe to attempt the bar ; but now that his own
launch had broken adrift from the stern of the
brig, and was cutting all kinds of capers in the
breakers, he wanted me to pick her up; but
finding that I did not wish to be under an
obligation to him, he sent his slaves out in a
cockle-shell of a thing, against which proceeding I strongly but unsuccessfully protested,
never expecting to see them again. However
poor darkie went, and managed to reach the
launch and bring her in with the flood-tide,
but lost the cockle-shell.

I remained on board the brig until half-flood,
when we steered her in with a boat on each
quarter, Parker taking the helm of the pinnace,
and I that of the barge, and it was with the
utmost difficulty that I persuaded them to make
sufficient sail to weather a sand bank, and even
as it was, a breaker curled up close to the stern
of the barge. Leaving her at Hippopotamus
Point, I took the Captain and Azvedo's brother
to the town, dined there, had a long chat with

Dr. Peters, and returned to the Point in the night. The following morning at daylight, I got over a smooth bar, and arrived on board, having been absent six days, heartily tired of sleeping in the boat, where anxiety and hard boards soon knocks one up. One night I started up about 2. A. M., declared it was daylight, and got under weigh, much to the discomfort of all hands, and had to anchor again for several hours ; all this in boats loaded with stock, water, fruit, &c., with a dangerous bar staring one in the face, is anything but agreeable, and requires a constitution of iron.

The Helena had sailed for Zanzibar during our absence, and I was much disappointed at not seeing more of my old friend and messmate, Charles Forsyth, whom I had just time to shake by the hand the day we anchored, when he came on board, after boarding our old friend the Domingo Cardoza from Mozambique. By her we were all much concerned to hear of the deaths of Moraes, the secretary, and Cardoza, the collector of customs. The former was universally esteemed as a most upright and just person, and to the latter's hospitality we

I

were indebted for three or four days' amusement at Carbaçeira.

We learnt from the Helena that she had taken the Governor-General to Mozambique, from Sofala, where he had been wrecked in the Caçadore, a small brig, and had written to the Governor of Quillimane to ask the assistance of the first English man-of-war that touched there. Poor old man, at his time of life, he ought to be quietly at home with a wife to take care of him, instead of cruising about amongst musquitoes and miasma, in a rotten old brig. So much for being an old batchelor!

We continued cruising between Luabo and the Macuzé, without seeing anything until the evening of November 8th, when about 9 P.M. I was packed off in a great hurry to board a brig, which proved to be the Domingo Cardoza from Quillimane once more. The old brute! many a chase has she given us, and such a thing in the shape of a vessel you never saw. She is like a coffin rose upon, and her channels are so close to the water that it requires not a little care to keep from under them. Her quarters are

overhung with chairs and tables the property
of the Banyan passengers, who always carry
their all with them. This splendid specimen of
African ship-building is generally called the
Biscoito, from the number of little leaks all
over her, and a stream of clear water is continually running from her pumps.

On November the 10th, we observed the
Juavo Adelaide coming out of the river, and
in the night I boarded her, and found that she
had got a new rudder, the iron work of which
had been made by a slave of Azvedo's, whose
brother I found on board ill with the fever,
and sent the boat back for O'Hagan, who
returned with Piers, and gave him some medicine. I learnt that Dr. Peters and the Governor had started for Senna on the 8th.

The following day the Bittern arrived from
the Cape, and we remained at anchor together
for two days, when she sailed for Inhamban,
in consequence of the information I had received at Quillimane: much to our regret,
Norman went in the brig, for in him we
lost a worthy and cheerful messmate.

On the 16th, I boarded the Portuguese

brig-of-war Don Juan de Castro, four days from Mozambique, on her way to Sofala for the stores and masts of the Caçadore; and as she was to remain on the coast for some time, Captain Wyvill thought it a good opportunity to complete our water, and we made sail for Majunga, where we arrived on the 22nd. We found at anchor here, the French corvette Zelée, and learnt from her that a French squadron, consisting of a line of battle ship, two steamers, and other vessels, had lately arrived at Nos Beh; and indeed their movements in these parts look very suspicious, for during her stay the corvette's boats were constantly sounding the anchorage, and making a careful survey of the whole place.

Caswell and myself were sent on shore to wait on the Governor and ascertain the facilities for watering: we were accompanied by Mamoudjee, who acted as interpreter, and on arriving at the gate of the fort, found it guarded as before, with a sentry on each side, their muskets meeting in the centre, so as to lock the bayonets which were not withdrawn, until permission was sent down from the Governor. We were received with a guard as before, "supporting arms," and, approaching the Governor hat in hand, were received with a hearty shake by the hand, and a sign to sit down. Caswell took the post of honour next to the Governor, and the interpreter sat opposite to us, about twelve officers ranging themselves in a half circle, dressed in their red coats and buttoned up to the chin. They seemed to have had a fresh importation from America lately, eagles, Massachusetts, and no end to States, figuring on their buttons.

The Governor commenced asking numerous questions, which Mamoudjee interpreted in the following style:—"The Governor, he ask how the captain been, and how all the officers been, since the ship been here last? How many places the ship go to, and what the news from all those places?" Eleven places were enumerated, which made them open their eyes. We told them of our disaster at Murderer's reefs, and the Governor expressed himself very sorry, but had no idea of the locality, and could not enlighten us as to who the people were. All he could say was, that they were not Ovas, but a race who would take a life for a pocket handkerchief.

We presented the captain's compliments, and offered to salute the Governor, if he would return it, and invited him to go on board. This, however, I understand, is out of his power, not only being against the orders of the Queen, but because also he is surrounded by spies and people, who, they fear, might take possession of the fort.

As soon as he found that we wanted twenty bullocks, the Governor invited the captain, Caswell, and myself, to dinner on the following day at *eleven o'clock*, which we accepted; and after discussing a bottle of champagne, we retired with the same honours, and on my way down I paid my friend the colonel a visit, whom I found laid up with the fever.

We found two wells near the beach, with good water; but they were so choked up with mud and stones, that the engine pumped them dry in a few minutes, and we were nearly starting for Nos Beh, when, on digging down about two feet, we came to a fine spring, which enabled us to get forty tons a day.

About half-past eleven we started for the fort, having been detained by a shower, and arrived about noon. The party consisted of the captain, Caswell, Alexander, Piers, O'Hagan, Marsh, and myself, and I was very sorry that I could not persuade Jack to go. We were received with the same honours as before, and the Governor and Captain were soon "hail fellow well met." The table was laid with a length of bed-ticking for a cloth, and a very good set of the old fashioned stone china, with deep oval dishes. In about a quarter of an hour, during which we had been seated according to our ranks, a large dish of rice was brought in covered with a white cloth, followed by a dish of curried fowl, which was served all round *à la soup*, and very good it was. Up and down the centre of the table were numerous black bottles, which proved to be excellent cherry brandy, and we had to drink it all dinner time, mixing it with water. The curry being removed, they brought in roast herons, and wild duck with spinach, and the kernel of the cashew-nut stewed as a vegetable. Behind each guest was a Sacalava girl, with a fan to keep the flies off: their features are rather good, with hair of the frizzly sort, between silk and wool, and apparently very populous, affording them ample employment for their nails; and my nymph appeared to tickle my ear, and go as near to my nose as possible, without touching it, to drive away the flies.

The Malagache part of the company expressed great admiration for Alexander's large bushy whiskers, and his neighbour kept continually feeling them, and declared, that could the Queen see him, he would be a great favourite. My right hand friend said to me:—"How he get waistcoats all the same dat: he shave plenty too much? me like waistcoats very much all the same dat." All eyes were fixed on poor Alec, and we had a hearty laugh, and he *nearly* blushed. After sitting for about an hour after dinner, we retired to the top of the house, which commands rather a pretty prospect. The guard were drawn up in the square under us, and I inquired how many soldiers the Governor had under his command, and was told that there were about 3,500 in the neighbourhood.

They are fine-looking men, and with their dark skins and white waistcloths look very picturesque. They are all armed with muskets and spears: the latter they plant in a line before them, and go through their drill with the English word of command. We expressed a wish to see them put through their facings, and after sundry lame attempts, all they could get through was shoulder and order arms: they gave the word " Rear rank, take close order," when they were already closed up, and *vice versâ;* plainly showing that their fine English word of command was all parrot work. However, they are not at all to be despised.

On the Monday, we commenced watering at 4 A.M., but heavy rains obliged us to leave off early in the afternoon. However, we got off eight of the bullocks, writing of which reminds me that the Governor, after dinner on Saturday, when he thought our hearts were open with his good cheer, tried to get the captain to give twelve, instead of ten dollars for each bullock, in which of course he was foiled, turning the laugh against himself. If he had succeeded, he would have deserved credit for making us pay for our dinners.

On Tuesday, we completed our water and bullocks, and sailed the next day ; but I must tell you a little more about this extraordinary people, before I get over again to our old cruising ground. On Sunday, we strolled about, and called on the Governor, who received us in an upstairs room, with open lattice work on each side, making it delightfully cool and pleasant. Here we discussed the exorbitant prices of fowls, rice, geese, and a bottle of Champagne, and his sable Excellency wanted very much to know if the captain and officers had any gold lace, epaulettes, or coats to sell, and he wanted one very large pair of epaulettes for grand occasions. He was dressed in a fustian shooting coat, nankin trousers, and a carpet cap, and is not at all a bad-looking man.

Whilst choosing the bullocks, one of the marines complained to me that one of the natives had stolen twenty-four handkerchiefs belonging to Alexander, and that one of the women knew the thief. I immediately told

Mamoudjee that unless the thief was found, and the property restored, I would have no more to do with him. Accordingly, soldiers were sent in all directions, and soon brought back the stolen goods and the culprit, who was a poor miserable diseased creature, covered with craw craw, and I certainly was not at all prepared to see him suffer so severely for his pilfering.

Arabs, Banyans, soldiers, and Malagaches got hold of some instrument of punishment ; cows' tails, strips of the palm leaf knotted, ropes' ends, and sticks were in great requisition, and used most unmercifully on the body of the almost naked wretch, as he was dragged to a post, and seized up by the hands, bleeding at the mouth, and crying most piteously, and I really thought they intended to beat the poor devil to death, and interfered, saying, that he had suffered enough, and was "plenty sick ;" but they said nobody dared let him go but myself, so I seized a clasp knife, and cut the seizings, telling him to be off and steal no more.

Soon after, the Governor came down with his

suite, and hearing what had happened, sent the culprit to the fort; and from what I heard I much feared they would cut his head off, so Lyall, and myself, earnestly begged the Governor to let him off; but he said the law must be carried into execution, promising, however, to convey our request to the Queen. On a subsequent visit, I found that the man died in the fort.

The Queen, they say, leads a most extravagant life, residing in a palace said to be of silver; but the truth I believe is, that it is a small place built by Radama, and thinly coated with silver. Her present favourite and prime minister is a sworn brother of the Governor of Majunga, they having cut each others' breasts, and tasted the blood; and after going through this ceremony, they risk life and everything else for each other. The heir to the throne is a lad about fifteen, and is about to make a tour round all the different Ova forts and possessions. A house has been built at Tenenerivo, twelve stories high, for which they have sent for large chandeliers from England or France.

I could find out very little about their religion. They admit the existence of a God, but seem to have very little idea of a future state. At one time, the missionaries made great progress; but claiming too many privileges for their converts, Christianity was forbidden under pain of death by the present Queen and her advisers. Many of the people still talk of Mr. Griffiths, who wrote a book in their language, and seems to have been a great favourite amongst them. Their soldiers have no pay, and when sick there is no hospital. The punishment for desertion is burning.

The morals of these people are at the lowest possible ebb; still they have some redeeming points; and however much they may endeavour to cheat in making a bargain, their hospitality, when once under their roof, is unbounded. I overheard an old sailor say, that they were never better treated in their lives; "for if you goes into their houses they axes you to sit down, and take the best they have, and that's more than they would do for you at Portsmouth or Plymouth, without making you pay." Just before

I went off to the ship, I sold my old coat for a bullock.

They have a great trade with the Americans, in hides and ebony. Marks, the American agent, ships annually 15,000 at a dollar each, for which they get three dollars in the States.

On November 27 we left Bembatooka Bay, and on the 1st of December were standing into Mozambique with a fair wind, and made so certain of being at anchor within the hour, that divine service was not performed; but on nearing the shore a strong current set us to the southward; and although under a heavy press of sail, going nine knots, we could not gain an inch, and the following morning shaped a course for Quillimane, where we arrived on the 5th, and boarded a small schooner from Mozambique, laden with lime. Alexander thinking her suspicious, I was sent to examine her papers, and found her commanded by an old acquaintance of mine, named Graças, who once paid me the compliment of wishing every Englishman but myself at the bottom of the Red Sea.

The following day I dined with the captain, and voluntered my services to go up
to the town for stock and information ; consequently, accompanied by Parker and O'Hagan,
I went on board the schooner on the 7th, and
made sail about 11 A.M. for the bar, with a
fine fair wind; but one little craft, being no
clipper, made but little progress, and the hot
tropical sun made us very thirsty, so we soon
had recourse to a hamper well stored with
beer, porter, rum, and a round of beef, the
effects of which were soon visible on Senhor
Graça, who began to see double, and kept
continually shouting, " Horsa, horsa," (Luff,
luff) ; and in three minutes we should have
been in the breakers, and reduced to vanishing
fractions, had I not made signals to the old
contre-maître, who was at the helm, and
piloted her in myself. My friend Horsa, horsa, soon lost his equilibrium, and remained
hors de combat until late in the evening, when
we anchored off the town, and I found, much
to my regret, that our friend Azvedo was gone
into the interior for fifteen days.

However, I landed, and had a palaver with his

blacks, and called on the old Governor, who had just returned from Chiponga, having been re-called from his Government, and superseded. From him I learnt the welcome intelligence that my friend Dr. Peters had arrived at Senna, in safety, and had started for Tete in good health. Having no offer of beds, I returned to the schooner, and we pigged it out in the least miserable way we could.

In the morning, Senhor Isidore, the collector of the customs, came on board, and begged us to take up our abode at his house, in the absence of our friend, which kind invitation we gladly accepted; but previous to going there, paid the new Governor, Manuel Abreu Madeira, a visit. We found him laid up in his bed with a severe fever, and exceedingly low; and very fortunately O'Hagan had taken up medicines with him, and undertook to set him on his legs again. We then breakfasted at Senhor Isidore's, who received us most hospitably, and made us quite at home, sending his blacks to wash our clothes and provide for all our wants.

In the evening, I went alone to see the

Governor, and found that he had not taken
the medicine we had sent him, fearing that
it might have passed through the hands of some
of the Portuguese, whose good will towards
him he much doubted from his avowed intention of suppressing the Slave Trade; but
on my assuring him that Dr. O'Hagan had
brought it from the ship and mixed it himself, he took it; and the good effects were
quite visible the next day, when I called and
had a long conversation with him respecting
the slave trade, which he professed to abomi-
nate, and determined to use all his power to
stop, at Quillimane. I assured him that
Captain Wyvill was most anxious to co-ope-
rate with the Portuguese authorities, and
afford him the assistance of Her Majesty's
ships under his command : however, he was
so weak, that the doctor forbid him to talk
and excite himself.

On calling on my old acquaintance Said
Hamza, he seemed much hurt that I had not
paid him a visit on the day of my arrival,
saying, "What for, my friend, no come see me
when I got something good to tell him?"

This speech, with a little mystery in his manner, soon made me suspect that he wished me to meet him half way—in fact, to offer him a bribe. In the meantime, an Arab came in, looking as if he was afraid that every piece of furniture in the room was going to spring up in testimony against him,—winking his eye, waving his hand, and begging me not to split on him if he told me something. He then asked me how much I would give him, and if I would get him a passage to Mozambique on his informing me how I could get hold of a slave. However, I forbore to compromise myself with him, and took it very coolly, plainly seeing that his and Said Hamza's were one and the same story; and after a little beating about the bush with the latter, I made an agreement.

And now I learnt that, fifteen days before, 800 slaves had marched from Quillimane for the River Mariangombe, off which was a brig at anchor waiting to ship them by means of a dow, which had been taken as a smuggler by the late Governor, and afterwards released and hired for this purpose. The captain of her had only left the town four days. Fortunately a brig was to sail the next morning for Inhamban, and I wrote a few lines by her to Captain Wyvill, who immediately on the receipt of my letter, got under weigh, and on the morning of the 13th discovered the brig at anchor off Mariangombe, and drove her on shore with 420 slaves on board, the particulars of which I will relate in a future page.

CHAPTER VII.

WISHING to make the most of our time and
see as much as possible of the interior, we
hired twenty blacks to carry us in machilas,
and on the 10th, started at six o'clock in
the morning with a double-barrelled gun,
and four bearers each. The novelty of the
whole thing put us in high spirits, and the
shouts and antics of the darkies kept us in a
roar of laughter. The first part of the path
was through a rich plain, well-cultivated, and
growing rice, calavances, and Indian corn. On
each side of this plain are mango, cashew, and
various sorts of the palm-trees in most luxuri-

ant foliage, now and then for a mile or so
affording the most delightful shade; but at
other places the grass was high and rank,
springing from an unhealthy swamp, and
swarming with myriads of musquitoes, which
made us pay toll as we passed.   We then got
into a flat monotonous country, the land all
burnt up and the path intersected with large
cracks, shewing that during the rainy season
it must be all under water.

Not a hill or the outline of a mountain can be
seen, and the only sign of man was the solitary
path we were travelling by.   Now and then we
met a party of blacks of from eight to twelve
wending their way towards the town with bun-
dles of dried meat, &c.: they invariably stepped
out of the road, clapped their hands twice,
and drew back their right feet.   The women put
their feet together, and making an inclination
by bending both knees with their arms crossed,
saluted us with a broad grin or sometimes a
half-fearful expression of countenance.   Many
of them had their children lashed to their
backs sleeping as comfortably as possible.

We travelled in this manner at the rate of

five miles an hour, now and then increasing to a regular run, with shouts and sudden exclamations. About every ten minutes the foremost bearers give three taps on the bamboo and the whole force lift the concern together over their heads and shift shoulders, and about every half hour a fresh set of bearers relieve them. Our cavalcade was most picturesque, the reserve all carrying something. One had a basket on his head, another a spear over his shoulder with a mat on it, or some strips of elephant's flesh. Fine, sleek, strong-built fellows they are, and from practice carry an immense weight, without galling their shoulders, for a whole day. They are not slaves, but Colonos from different tribes in the interior, who settle in the Portuguese possessions, and let themselves out as machila bearers, labourers, &c. After going about ten miles, we came to a grove of mango, cocoa-nuts, and cashew-trees, where we hove-to and breakfasted, our kind host having provided for our inward man, in the shape of cold meat, bread, wine and *gin;* but more than all these, we enjoyed the nice cool milk of the green cocoa-nuts which our bearers brought to us with the tops nicely sliced off.

In about half an hour we again made a start, but the path became so narrow that we only had two bearers at a time, and had they been slaves I should not have felt at all easy. Even as it was we frequently got out and walked a mile or two, or started off to the right or left to shoot birds. Nothing occurred to change the scene of this low flat country but an occasional ridge of trees and now and then a glimpse of the river, and about 10 A.M. we found ourselves amongst the huts of a village built on piles about six feet from the ground, on the banks of the river Licuara, which during the rainy season is so swollen, that the blacks have to paddle amongst their huts in canoes.

We found it to be one of the stations of the Praço of Senhor Morgado, who had a great number of men cutting wood to build the largest house at Quillimane, and was expecting us. He gave us a most hearty welcome, and soon produced from a large chest all the necessaries for a most excellent breakfast, which consisted

of curry, snow-white rice, fish, all kinds of preserves, mangoes, and capital wine, the more
acceptable and surprising from being produced
in one of the most miserable-looking places
one can well conceive.

The sun was scorchingly hot, and we could
not well venture out without an umbrella, and
after resting for about an hour watching the
blacks launching several large cargoes down a
muddy bank, which was so slippery that
they carried away painters and floated quietly
down the stream by themselves, we prepared
to cross the river,—and a most laughable scene
it was. Our machilas with their bearers got
over first in an immense canoe made of a
single tree hollowed out; and there they were
floundering about, above their middles in mud,
yelling, grinning, and struggling with all their
might to waddle up the bank. On our side the
mud was so deep that a man could scarcely
move by himself, but we got one by one on
two fellows' shoulders, who floundered down to
the edge of the canoe and dropped us in,
when we had to sit in the bottom to keep her
from capsizing. On the opposite side a small

canoe was let down the bank with a rope attached to it, and we were drawn up separately into a thick jungle, where we had to creep under branches and cross streams over the broken limbs of trees, after which we came to another station consisting of a few huts. Here we saw a poor unfortunate wretch eaten up with leprosy : he was a fine-looking black, about six feet three inches high, and stout in proportion, doomed to die aloof from and shunned by his fellow men.

We now went on at a slapping pace, having no inducement to stop, in the shape of scenery, until we again came to the bank of the river, where there was a ford waist-deep, which the blacks crossed, carrying the machilas over their heads whilst we got into a small canoe ; and after sundry narrow escapes from turning over, while being tracked down by two darkies, we landed on the same bank of the river, having merely taken this route to avoid a large swamp.

The country now became more interesting, being partially wooded and higher. The path lay along the bank of the river,

K

and every now and then we got a shot at
many-coloured birds, and occasionally heard
the rustling of gazelles and other animals.
About 4 P.M. we came in sight of the establishment, situated in the midst of a great
number of immense ant-hills from twenty to
thirty feet high, and fifty to sixty in circum-
ference at the bottom, with trees growing out
of the sides and top.   The scene was a most
novel one, and when about a quarter of a
mile off, we all got into our machilas, and
were met by two drums and a fife, the performers on which marched before us with the
greatest gravity, playing a row-de-dow up to
the gates of a large white building, where the
Portuguese flag was flying.   We now entered
a vast square, in the midst of which was a
large neat pigeon-house, and we were all
struck with the good order and regularity of
the whole place.

On the left was a nice-looking dwelling-
house ; on the right a large store-house, the
walls of which were loopholed, and about
two feet thick. Opposite the gate was a
comfortable building for the working slaves,

and here and there, in good order, were several pieces of cannon which had formerly belonged to the American corvette Concorde. Morgado told us that he intended to wall and loophole the place all round as a protection against independent tribes of blacks and wild beasts.

At sunset the drums beat, the people are mustered, and the colours hauled down, and the gates are closed. The married blacks live in huts outside, which are barricadoed all round with stakes and branches to protect them from lions, which are very numerous and constantly prowling about, walking off now and then with a stray woman or child.

We sat down to a most sumptuous dinner and found our host a very amusing person. Could we have spoken the language more fluently, I might have got much interesting information from him. His property is larger than the whole of Portugal, and contains 30,000 inhabitants, a great part slaves, the rest colonos: it produces yearly 280 arobas of ivory.

The elephants are generally caught during the rainy season when overtaken by the floods, and either drowned, shot, or speared. The country has immense resources within itself, producing iron, copper, and the precious metals. Coal is abundant and good, but too far from the river to be available for steam navigation, except during the floods, when the river is navigable all the way from Tete, a distance of 260 leagues. Much might be done by a company who would pay the Governors well enough to induce them to discountenance the slave and contraband trades; but at present the demoralized state of society is beyond description. A custom-house without duties, a judge without justice, a church without a priest, bribery, peculation, and disease, go hand in hand with slavery and grasping avarice. Good health is a thing unknown to them, and their faces are the colour of gold. They heap up but never live to enjoy in their own country.

An instance of the way in which the revenue is defrauded was told me by Morgado. It appears that the brig Uniâo, under Portuguese colours, anchored off the bar, and wished to enter his manifest at the custom-

house. "No," said the Governor, "unless you
give me 3,000 dollars you shall not come up
the river." The captain refused, the brig
remained off the bar, and the people of Quillimane sent down their launches, loaded them,
and landed the cargo without paying a far-
thing of duty. But as these things are all well
known and publicly talked about amongst
themselves, the Governor never goes without a
due proportion of eye-water to make him wink.

The history of this vessel is a curious one,
and as she has made a great stir in these seas
since we have been out, I shall give you a
faint outline of her career. When the Cor-
corde was wrecked at the Macuzé she was at
Quillimane fully equipped and waiting for a
slave cargo, but was hired by the American
officers to convey them and their crew to Rio.
On crossing the bar she was boarded by Craw-
ley in the Lily's boat, who would have made
a prize of her, and much offended the Americans by detaining her; and they swore, "By
gor! that heaven and earth had combined
against them." However, she took them safely
across, and on the way the captain amused

them by relating various anecdotes of his slave voyages, bragging of having thrown some overboard, flogged others to death, &c., with marks of great satisfaction. She then went to Lisbon and took in a cargo for the coast, obtaining from the Portuguese Government a special license to trade at a reduced duty in all the ports on the East Coast of Africa, where she collected a great quantity of ivory, and then to complete her cargo went to Madagascar for rice, with which she returned to Mozambique, and endeavoured to get the Governor-General to allow her to land it and re-ship it that they might take it home as colonial produce. After this she was seized off Quillimane by the Helena and Bittern, and sent to the Cape for a breach of the slave treaty, having taken on board several blacks at Mozambique in a very irregular kind of way, and having a number of suspicious fittings about her. However, she was liberated by the Mixed Commission, and the captors were cast in heavy damages, which they refused to pay and protested against the whole proceedings, so that I suppose we shall hear more of it.

Amongst the passengers taken was our old acquaintance Carmache (of "*coup de pistolet*" notoriety,) and he got for his detention 300*l.*, a larger sum than he would have made in six years by following his trade of smuggling spirits amongst the Arabs at Nos Beh. The captain, Morgado told me, was well known as a most accomplished rascal, having formerly commanded a slaver for a person at Rio, and getting safely across with his cargo, he sold it on his own account at Pernambuco, and made off with the money to Lisbon.

In this kind of conversation we passed away an hour or two over our wine; and going out to take a little fresh air, our kind host warned us not to go out of the candle-light, as a stray lion might make a small mouthful of us; and you may depend we did not require a second caution. Three beds were made up for us in a small room, and, as is the custom in these countries, every window was shut to keep out the night-air and musquitoes, making it frightfully close and hot. I got up in the night, and opened the door, and was much amused with the scene before

me. By the light of a flickering lamp, I
beheld about a dozen black boys stretched out
on a bit of mat, looking like a heap of arms
and legs with a ball of black wool sticking up
every here and there. They were sleeping so
soundly, that I walked about the room without causing one of them to stir, and returned
to my bed feverish and excited, longing for
daylight, which no sooner dawned, than I
jumped up and ordered a basin of cold water,
and after a refreshing wash, sallied out to
explore. Soon after, we got coffee, and after
visiting a very nice vegetable garden, took a
stroll with our guns, but were soon driven in
by the sun. Parker and O'Hagan, however,
could not resist a cruise along the banks of
the river, and whilst they were away I had a
long chat with Morgado about the slaves.
Several of the boys were before the door
rubbing each other with cocoa-nut oil, and I
remarked that several of them were branded
either on the breast or arm. These, it appears,
are brought from the interior, children born
on the estate never being marked. Morgado
complained that the Majogos, or natives of

Anjozha, constantly ascended the rivers in dows, and carried off all the blacks they could lay their hands on, with impunity, as it would take thirty days to visit all the stations on his estate, travelling nine miles a day.

About thirty or forty people were making bricks, and I have often been highly amused at watching the process. In the first place a pit is dug, and a quantity of clay thrown into it with a proportion of water. Boys of from eight to twelve years old are sent into this to work it up with their feet, which they do in measured time, laying their hands on each other's shoulders, and stamping together with their right foot to a chorus of "Whow! Whow! Whow!" When of a proper consistency, the clay is worked up into about ten-inch balls, and each boy carries one on his head to a shed, where the women form the bricks in moulds, and place them out to dry. A large round pile of fire-wood is then laid, and the bricks are baked in the open air. I never saw a stone of the smallest size in the whole country.

About 1 P.M. I was roused from a comfortable nap, and found the whole establishment in commotion, and we were soon going along at a brisk trot in our machilas, preceded as before by the two drums and a fife. We returned by a much straighter road than we came by, and had to cross several branches of the river in small canoes, which was at times a long and rather hazardous proceeding, our company consisting of upwards of fifty people, and we could form a capital idea of the mode of travelling in this country. Morgado explained everything to us on the road, kept us well supplied with *frigidum sine*, and about 7 P.M. we entered the town, our bearers as fresh as when they started, singing, howling, and cheering each other up. So ended one of the most interesting excursions I have ever undertaken, showing me, as it did, not only the general face of the country, but the mode of travelling and living, and the manner in which the blacks are kept under. I must, in justice, say, that I never, during my frequent visits to Quillimane, saw a single instance of cruelty beyond the un-English-

looking practice of chaining numbers of naked
wretches together by the neck.

At Senhor Isidore's I found Hornby, who
had come up in charge of the barge, and had
boarded the brig, with my letter on board
inside the bar, which of course made me very
anxious, fearing that the slave-brig might get
in her cargo, and be off; but it was impossible
to get down that night, so, after calling on the
Governor, whom we found much better, we
supped with Morgado, and slept soundly without rocking until daylight, when I sallied out
to prepare for a start, collecting stock, and
paying our bearers, for which purpose I purchased eight pieces of blue dungaree at two
dollars and a half a piece, paying each man
four fathoms, which they told me was much
more than any but Englishmen would have
given them. However, I thought it little
enough for being carried thirty-five miles one
day, and twenty the next, and gave them
something in addition to drink with.

After purchasing two casks of wine and a
great quantity of stock, I found that my boat
would not hold half of it, with the presents

which were sent down for our Christmas dinner from all the principal persons of the place.
The Governor sent us a cask of Madeira;
Morgado, six pigs, twelve large Muscovy ducks,
and two sheep; Velozo, four sucking pigs;
Azvedo, fowls, bread, and eggs; Senhor Isidore,
four dozen of wine, two casks of mangos, with
roast fowls, and wine and gin for the passage
down. So I was obliged to determine on
leaving Parker, O'Hagan, and the wash-
clothes behind; and after a grand dinner at
Senhor Velozo's, I went to Senhor Isidore's to
take leave, just as the pilot came in, after
taking the brig over the bar with my letter.
I was not a little pleased to hear that the
Cleopatra had made sail to the northward
under a heavy press of canvass, as soon as the
boat returned from boarding her: perhaps it
was mere fancy, but I thought that they all
seemed to have a shrewd suspicion that there
was something in the wind. However, I put a
good face on the matter, and started for Hippopotamus Point as if I expected the ship to
stand in the next morning, when we ran into
a creek, landed and fed the stock; and

Hornby and myself took possession of Senhor Isidore's house, which we found in charge of a Portuguese, who could not do too much for us.

On the 14th, I was obliged to run up to the town for spirits for the boat's crew, and found every thing in *statû quo*, although they appeared rather uneasy, and I returned to the Point the same night. Old Brown, my coxswain, could not make out my movements at all, and expressed his wonder where the ship could be; and when I told him it was all right, his look was one I shall never forget or cease to laugh at whenever I call it to mind, as he exclaimed, " Ah, sir, you'm up to snuff *you* be!" I spent the following day looking out anxiously for the ship, and in the evening a brig anchored off the bar under Portuguese colours, and I made arrangements to pounce upon her the next morning, hoping to make a prize of her; but at daylight, just before sunrise, I had the felicity of seeing the masts of my own ship in strong relief against the blushing sky, which gave me time to take in my stock, and proceed quietly on board. The brig had hoisted a pendant, and proved to be the Don Juan de Castro, so I dropped the pilot on board, as we passed his boat, not being able to get out.

On arriving on board, I had the satisfaction of finding that my information had proved correct, and that the ship, the morning after receiving my note, had observed a brig at anchor off the river Mariangombe, unfortunately dead to windward. About 20 minutes past 9, a boat was observed to leave her, and immediately afterwards she made sail and stood for the shore, and at 11 o'clock grounded, when another boat left her. The cutters were immediately armed and sent away under Alexander, whilst the ship anchored as close in as she could with safety, in six fathoms, and the pinnace was sent with two kedges and three hawsers, to endeavour to get her off; but at half-past four the boats were observed to be returning, and Mr. Caswell went in the galley to see what could be done. At 10 p.m. he returned with all the boats, having been unable to approach the brig over which the sea was making a clean breach. When Alexander first got on board in the cutter, he found that her crew had deserted her, leaving the steward and supercargo sick in the bunks on deck, with 420 slaves, the greater part under hatches, fastened down with spike nails, and left by the merciless wretches to be drowned or smothered. Never was there a more dreadful attempt at cool, deliberate, and wholesale murder; and yet there is no means of punishing the perpetrators; no judge nor magistrate residing at Mozambique, and the judge at Quillimane being a coloured man, formerly a gentleman's servant, and one of the greatest slave-dealers in the place. Never was an officer placed in a more awkward position, the cutters being all but stoved, and there appearing every chance of the brig's being knocked to pieces as the tide went down. Alexander thought the best plan was to allow them to swim on shore, and the greater part of them reached it in safety. On the two following days, the boats were employed in completing the destruction of the brig by fire, and brought on board the two sick Portuguese and seven negroes who had remained on board. A few bodies were found on the beach and buried.

On being measured, the vessel proved to be 300 tons, and quite capable of carrying 800 slaves. After remaining on board a few hours, I was again sent to the town, accompanied by Alexander, with the two prisoners. I found the place in a great ferment, as they had heard of the destruction of the brig about one o'clock that day, and the Governor had sent Senhor Velozo to the Mariangombe, and planted soldiers in all the paths leading to the town, to pick up the slaver's crew as they came in. He seemed to be in a great state of excitement, and would have it that he was disgraced, so I took leave of him, fearing that in his then weak state he might have a relapse.

I again took up my quarters at Senhor Isidore's, and all our friends were as civil as ever, although I know that several of them were deeply engaged in the slave trade, and had sustained considerable loss by the destruction of the brig. In fact, they seem to consider it a fair game of chance between us.

The next morning, soon after daylight, I visited Said Hamza, and paid him thirty sovereigns for his information. What a fright he was in! and how I laughed at his ludicrous speeches, such as, "Now, Mr. Barnard, you make your face white, all the same as if you hear nothing; and s'pose anybody ask you if Said Hamza tell you anything; you say, He, poor fellow! what he know? I not ask him."

In the evening he was sitting in the porch at Senhor Isidore's, when I popped upon him unexpectedly, and his confusion was beyond all description. He changed colour like a chameleon, and looked black, blue, yellow, and green by turns, which highly amused me after his morning lecture.

In the course of the day I as usual wandered about, whilst the Portuguese were taking their siesta, fishing for information, and in the course of conversation with the person from whom I had been in the habit of purchasing stock, I found that she had been accused of telling me about the brig, and I immediately pointed out to her how much better it would be if she really would give me information, and pocket a good round sum of money instead of bearing all the odium without the reward; and I promised to call again in the evening after she had had time to consider and consult with her friend, whom I had kept a look out on for some time, knowing he was rather a loose fish. Accordingly, I found them, when I called, in deep consultation, and after a little beating about the bush they consented to inform me from time to time of the movements of the slaves, which are constantly kept in readiness in the neighbourhood of Quillimane, to march to any point where a vessel might appear. This would give a cruiser ample time, as they could not get off under several days. They also told me that a large ship called the Hannibal was daily expected off Luabo, fitted to take in 1,500 slaves.

CHAPTER VIII.

I ARRIVED on board on the 18th, and we
made sail immediately for Mozambique, where
we anchored on the 21st inside the fort. On
the same day Parker had a severe attack of
fever, most probably brought on by exposure
to the night air in the Quillimane River, and
sleeping with his face in the sun on our way
off. As soon as we anchored, I was sent on
shore with letters to the Governor-General,
and to endeavour to get water; but I found
the Government tanks were all under repair,
and we eventually had to purchase it at a dollar

a ton. The next day (Sunday) I went with Lyall up the river to look at some bullocks, and after a long pull and sail in a burning sun, landed at a dilapidated building which had evidently been once a large establishment; but now the presses, tanks, &c., were in a confused mass of ruins. A small table was placed outside the door of an outhouse, and a great number of mangoes were placed before us, which after our pull were very refreshing. Each of us must have eaten at least a dozen and a half; after which we walked out to examine the bullocks, and offered twenty-five dollars each for ten of them, but their owner wanted a most exorbitant price and took the sulks, so we made the best of our way to the country-house of Senhor Nobré, who gave us a capital dinner and sold us ten bullocks.

We did not get on board until nine, and at half-past two in the morning I landed with the barge and pinnace to send off water, and remained on shore all day knocking about in the sun; after which I dined in the cabin to meet the Governor, and sat up until nearly midnight. The next day I felt rather unwell, refused to

dine out, and kept quiet; and on Christmas-
day had the morning-watch. At daylight the
pilot came on board, and we got under weigh
with a light breeze, and in the act of wearing
the ebb-tide we were driven on shore under
the fort, and there left on our broadside. Before
eight a heavy tropical shower drenched me to
the skin, and, without shifting, I remained on .
the forecastle, in one of the most scorching suns
I ever felt, for two or three hours; getting a
bower-anchor under the pinnace, a work of
much difficulty from the awkward position of
the ship.

After this I felt much exhausted, and
went below to breakfast, but found I could
not eat, and drank off a glass of ale, and
then had to lie down with a most splitting headache. However, after Lyall had
bathed my head with cold water, I rallied
and went on deck until noon, when I was
obliged to give in, and go on the sick
list. At four the ship was hove off and
got to sea, and in the evening the mids
and officers sat down to their Christmas
dinner in the gun-room, and a miserable one

it was, as they were all thoroughly fagged out.

. On the 27th, after two nights of dreadful suffering, I had all the symptoms of a severe fever, and Captain Wyvill kindly had a cot slung for me in his own cabin, and I was bled for the first time in my life. For many days .I was in a most dreadful state, and every half-hour seemed a day: strange fancies. haunted me, and I could not bear to be left alone. An idea that I should die now and then came over me, and poor Jack could not bear to hear me talk about it and was obliged to leave me.

We had in the meantime anchored off Luabo, and the weather was sultry with torrents of rain until the 3rd of January, when the Sappho rejoined us, and took Parker on board for the Cape Hospital; but I was not well enough to be removed to a strange vessel and preferred remaining on board my own ship, where under the kind and skilful treatment of Dr. Kettle, and Drs. Piers and O'Hagan, I got gradually better, and on the 17th of January, managed to creep about and appreciate the blessing of returning health.

Nothing could exceed the kindness and atten--
tion of Captain Wyvill, who kept me at his
table long after I was convalescent, and treated
me quite as a son, providing every comfort and
luxury he could think of; and for all these
blessings, I trust I am sincerely thankful to an
ever-watchful and beneficent Providence.

During my illness the boats made two trips
up the river, in charge of Hornby, and I
received sundry kind notes from my Portuguese
friends, regretting that there was a prospect
of not seeing me again. On February 9th, I
heard from my friend Dr. Peters, who had been
very fortunate in making friends with people
who afforded him every facility, and enabled
him to reach Tete in twenty-one and a-half
days. He described the country as being very
beautiful, with mountains not nearly as high as
they are generally supposed to be. The climate
of Tete was exceedingly damp, but on the
whole healthy; and he found some consolation
for the want of society in the attention and
civility of the inhabitants and the great success
he met with in his researches. Continual wars
not far from the town, destroy what has been

gained by agriculture and commerce, and heads are stuck up on poles in every direction. For unless a white man be present, no quarter is given on either side, and, such is the state of things, that a man may run a knife into his neighbour without its even being inquired into.

Hyænas and tigers enter through the breaches of the simple stone wall, and carry away the blacks from the very thresholds of the houses; and crocodiles constantly sieze the negresses who go into the River Zambesi to wash. Their houses are covered with straw, for they are too lazy to make tiles. The principal commerce is in ivory, and the slave trade is gradually diminishing. The quantity of gold-dust said to be exported is much exaggerated, every one's ideas in this country being concentrated on riches.

Dr. Peters intended, if possible, to penetrate farther into the interior, and endeavour to do something for the unhappy blacks, by making some arrangement with their principal oppressor; for he says, it is a pitiful sight to see a whole nation destroyed without having done any wrong.

The slaves that are brought from the interior
are poor half-starved looking creatures, attached
to each other by ropes round the neck; and
famine is spreading its ravages throughout this
ill-fated country. The province is in such a
state of decay, that it cannot continue long
under its present government, and a more
powerful one would scarcely risk the expense
and loss of life attendant upon the many
changes that must take place before it could
be bettered.

We left Quillimane on February 10th, and
on the 16th, anchored off Majunga, in company with the American barque, Orb, from
Zanzibar, where eight days before, she had left
a brig under Tuscan colours, which had been
sold at Mauritius, and sailed from thence with
a pass of four months. I immediately sug-
gested to the captain, that this must be the
same brig reported in May last, as having made
her appearance off the River Luabo, under Sardinian colours, and which lost her captain and
boat's crew. At first he seemed rather inclined
to go after her, but on reading the Tuscan
Treaty—which is on the same basis as the

L

French, and does not allow us to interfere with
their vessels, unless within thirty leagues of
Madagascar—the idea was given up. For many
miles outside Bembatooka Bay, the whole face
of the ocean was covered with uprooted trees,
masses of rushes and branches from the banks
of the river; and on one branch we saw an
unfortunate chameleon drifting quietly out to
sea, and we had much difficulty in making
head against the strong current that was setting out of the bay.

. We found the wells full of water, and completed in two days, and the purser being sick,
I purchased twenty-three bullocks for him, and
two large bulls to take as a present to Azvedo.
But although it was the very best season, not
a vegetable was to be had, and this is a country
capable of producing everything. The Ova
soldiers cultivate nothing but rice, and keep
the Sacalavas in such a state of subjection, that
they cannot call an inch of ground their own.

On the 20th we left Majunga, and on
the 26th fell in with Her Majesty's brig
Bittern, off the River Mariangombe, and on
the following day anchored off Quillimane,

in company.   The next morning I started
for the town, in charge of the barge and
pinnace, Jack taking the latter, with the two
bulls on board, whilst I called for any of the
Bitterns who would like to go.   Chaloner and
Dr. Burns accompanied me, and we arrived at
4 P. M., against a strong ebb-tide.   Azvedo
had arrived from the Macuzé only the day
before, and received us in his usual kind manner, and was much astonished and delighted
with the bulls, which were the admiration of
the whole place.

I found the Governor quite recovered and
talking twenty to the dozen, and I had a long
conversation with him respecting the state of
the country, and he complains most bitterly of
its impoverished and wretched state, and the
impossibility of ameliorating it without funds,
which it is out of the power of the Portuguese
Government to supply.

The ex-Governor, Don Fernando Carlos de
Costa, was on his death-bed, and never did
I see a more perfect wreck of a man.   Worn
down to a mere skeleton, the natural cling-
ing to life was still strong within him, and

L 2

he talked of soon being on his way to Lisbon.
At other times he was quite incoherent, and
they say that his recall by his Government
preyed on his mind, and brought him down
more than any bodily disease.   Dr. Burns did
everything in his power to alleviate his sufferings, but without the slightest hope of restoring
him to health.

The evening before we left, the Governor
gave us a soirée, and I had a long chat with
his wife, who is a very pleasing and lady-like
person; and during the illness of her husband,
I had often remarked her devoted attention
and constant anxiety.   Their story is rather
a romantic one.   It appears that he was
lodging at the house of her mother, who was a
person in humble circumstances at Lisbon, and
he was laid up with a very painful and severe
illness, during which the daughter attended on
him, and on his recovery he married her, and
she has since followed his fortunes, or rather
misfortunes, through various changes, and has
at last brought up at that pest-house, Quillimane, which I fear will soon terminate both
their sufferings in this world.

Senhora Velozo was also of the party: she is the heiress whom I have before mentioned as having brought her husband a large house and a thousand slaves as a dowry. Soon after our arrival on the station, he took me over his house, which is certainly the best in Quillimane, and exultingly said, "This is rather better than being a prisoner on board the Crescent at Rio for slaving." I thought to myself, "every comfort in this world is certainly comparative, and I envy you neither of your delightful situations."

But I am sure you will by this time be tired of reading so much of one place, and as this was my last visit, I shall merely wind up with a few anecdotes of one or two dealers in human flesh, whose careers were interrupted through the information with which I had from time to time furnished the Captain.

I was sitting one evening in the porch of Azvedo's house, and asked Chaloner if he had any objection to take a Portuguese gentleman to the Cape, as I had before got him a passage in the Sappho, which, through my illness, he had missed. He was also a friend of Azvedo's

and Isidore's, both of whom have always shewn
the greatest hospitality to English officers.
No sooner had we agreed to take him, than I
was regularly besieged by people wishing to
get to Rio.   One man's cool impudence highly
amused me.   He commenced in tolerably good
English to converse about my bills which he
volunteered to cash in doubloons, saying, " I
have, Sir, several hundred doubloons which I
brought from Rio to buy ivory, and I am an
ivory merchant, but find that I can buy nothing
but blacks in this place.   Now, I do not like
that trade and am anxious to get to Rio again,
and if you could get me a passage in the Bittern I should be very much obliged."   I told
him that it was impossible, and that I had
only been induced to ask my Captain for a
passage for Isidore's friend, as a small return
for the hospitality the English officers had
received at his hands.   At this stage of our
conversation Azvedo called me on one side
and cautioned me not to have anything to do
with my applicant, as he was the captain of
the brig we had driven on shore, and who had
so *humanely* nailed down 400 of his fellow-

creatures to perish, with two of his partners in crime, who were sick in the bunks.

Another calico-renting looking individual, not satisfied with my refusal, demanded my reasons, saying that it was very hard that he should be left there to die. I cut him precious short, and told him that an English man-of-war was neither a passage nor an hospital ship, and that I did not want any discussion on the subject. I afterwards learnt that this man was secretary to Major Campos, whose slaves were actually on board the brig we had destroyed, so I considered myself very fortunate in having given him the cold shoulder. What a laugh they would have had at me, had they succeeded!

As the principal object of all my visits to the town was to gain information respecting the movements of the slave-dealers and their agents, I was obliged to be constantly on the *qui vive*, and found myself both suspected and watched since the affair of the brig. However, I managed to get the following, bit by bit, from various quarters.

Paulo Roderigue, the captain of the Defensivo, and the shipper of 1,800 slaves at Inhamban and Delagoa Bay, was again expected at the former place, in two or three months, for 800 blacks, which were in readiness. He was to have two American brigs under their own colours, one of which was to be delivered over to the slave-dealers, whilst the other was to take both American crews on board, touch at Quillimane with money to pay the authorities, who have been in the habit of conniving at the slave trade, and return to Rio; so you may easily conceive what little chance there is of putting down this detestable traffic, whilst the star-spangled banner, that boasted flag of liberty, waves over and protects the miscreants, to put down whom England has expended so many hundreds of lives of her bravest, and so many millions of treasure. Look at the results.

There are now at Quillimane and its neighbourhood 2,700 poor wretches for embarkation. Their owners are at Rio, 800 belonging to Manuel Pinto de Fonseca; 200 to Tavares, or Tavash; 2,000 to Bernadino de Sá. Only one slave agent remained at Quillimane, named Martinhas, and he intended to leave for Rio in the American.

Of the 420 slaves allowed to swim on shore from the brig off Mariangombe, 110 were retaken, and the rest were supposed to have escaped into the interior. She had on board five officers, four of whom had died of fever since her destruction. Eight of her crew were taken and sent to Mozambique in the Don Juan de Castro, and the captain and steward remained at Quillimane, most probably soon to be victims of the approaching sickly season.

Almost all communication has been cut off by our cruisers, and I was hailed with delight whenever I paid Quillimane a visit, and brought anything in the shape of news, although they must have been well aware that I had means of ascertaining their movements; and never have I visited a country where English officers seem to be more respected or receive more courtesy and hospitality than at Quillimane; and although I am heartily glad that this is likely to be my last visit, I shall long remember Senhor Azvedo, and three or four others, whom I shall be glad to hear of as being in some spot, the name of which does not convey to

L 3

the mind slavery, fever, and debased human nature, as does Quillimane.

After a very uncomfortable night at Hippopotamus Point in the boats, we got on board on the 3rd of March about noon, and found that the Helena had arrived from the Cape, bringing late and welcome letters from dear old England. No one that has not been on this miserable coast month after month, cruising from one point to another under easy sail, without seeing a vessel or the least novelty to change the horrid monotony, can fully appreciate the happiness of receiving unexpected intelligence of all we hold most dear on earth. In fact, letters are the only connecting links between us and the world, and enable us to bear every kind of privation in the hope of eventually realizing the joyful anticipations which the magic word "home" raises in our hearts. How often has it infused into me when down-hearted, fresh spirit to persevere during the long and weary eighteen years that I have been a wanderer on the face of the waters. What, indeed, should we do without Hope?

On the following day we weighed in com-

pany with the Helena and Bittern, and leaving
them on their way to Mozambique, we stood
to the southward to watch Luabo; and, as
the Bittern was to go to the Cape immediately,
we sent all our letters.   I little dreamt of
being there eighteen days before her.

About 3 A. M., on the 16th of March we
observed a sail on the weather beam, which
answered our flashes with a light, and kept company with us under easy sail until four, when
we wore, and she stood on, of which we took
but little notice, fancying it was the Bittern;
and it was not until daylight that we discovered her to be a merchant-vessel and made
all sail in chase.   As she did not attempt to
get away we soon closed her, and were sadly
puzzled when she showed her colours (red,
yellow, and white) which none of us had ever
seen before, and on boarding her about seven,
I found her to be the Pachetto de Monte
Video, manned by British subjects.

They told me the colours were Italian, but
seemed to be very doubtful as to what part of
Italy they belonged to, and on descending to
the cabin, I found that this was the very brig

that the Orb had given us information of at Majunga. I examined her papers, and found that she was cleared out from the Mauritius by a paper signed by the collector of customs at Port Louis, giving the foreign brig, Pachetto de Monte Video, permission to proceed to sea with stores and provisions for four months. This the captain and M. Manoe appeared to consider as a pass protecting them for four months; and, although it was dated five months previously, they held it as valid until four months had elapsed from the date of her leaving Port Louis.

The other papers consisted of a bill of sale from the Admiralty Court, and the usual certificate from the police and port officers, with an original pass in Italian from the Lucchese consul at Monte Video, all under the seal of the custom-house at Port Louis. I saw at once that there had been great irregularity, but did not consider that there were grounds sufficient to detain her on, for a breach of the slave treaty, so returned to my ship, and reported the whole of the circumstances to Captain Wyvill, who immediately ordered me to return

and bring her to an anchor close to the Cleopatra, which I did, and took the captain and
supercargo, with their papers, on board, on
examining which, the Captain determined to
send her to the Cape, and I was ordered to
take charge of her, and kindly allowed to take
my brother with me. A day was taken to
survey her, and we found by her log and the
admission of the master and crew that she had
sailed from Port Louis with a slave-cargo on
board, which they had got rid of at Madagascar, fearing it might compromise them if
they fell in with a man-of-war.

Her history is a curious one, and worth
relating. She sailed from Monte Video, the
beginning of 1844 ; cleared out for Viareggio,
the seaport of Lucca, and found her way to
Rio Janeiro and Santos, at the latter of which
places she probably took in her slave-cargo,
with which she arrived in May at Luabo or
some of the rivers in the neighbourhood, and
lost her captain and boat's crew in attempting
to cross the bar. One man only escaped, whom
I have frequently met at Quillimane. He was
a half-witted Italian who got a precarious kind

of living by singing, dancing, and playing Tom-
fool before the doors of the Portuguese merchants.

After this the brig was not heard of until
some months, when she was brought into Port
Louis, by the mate of an American whaler,
who fell in with her off Port Dauphin on the
south end of Madagascar.   Not knowing in
what part of the world she was, and in distress,
he agreed to navigate her for sixty dollars.
She was then fully equipped for the slave
trade, having plank, water-casks, farina, rice,
and beans, on board.   On arriving at Mauritius
she was seized and sold by the Admiralty
Court to pay her expenses and the seamen's
wages, and her cargo was landed at the custom-
house and bought with her at a public auction
by an English subject, who coppered and fitted
her out, re-shipped her cargo from the customs,
and sent her to Zanzibar, still under her
original colours, although British property, to
be sold, or sailed under the Arab flag. Some
misunderstanding took place with the Imaun,
and she eventually went to Mozambique and
Quillimane, off which latter place we captured

her nearly twelve months after we had received information of her having been on the coast.

I found M. Manoe, the supercargo, a very decent sort of fellow, and quite indignant at being supposed to be engaged in the slave trade. He had taken his passage on board, and offered to act as supercargo, that he might be enabled to arrange some mercantile transactions in which he had been engaged along the coast, when he unfortunately fell into our clutches. I made him caterer of the mess, and everything went on smoothly during a most prosperous passage to Simon's Bay, of a fortnight. Here I encountered numerous difficulties, and our cause was considered a very bad one. However, the attorney-general saw through it immediately, and said it was a very good case to bring before the Admiralty Court, and I set to work with the proctor; and in a few days applied to Sir John Wylde for a monition, which he for some time positively refused, not seeing on what grounds we had detained her. The various slave treaties were read over and over again, and a fortnight elapsed before I could get her into court, where the attorney-general soon set them all to rights, and left no doubt on my mind as to the result, although the judge and not a few of the lawyers were dead against me. After this another anxious fortnight passed away, at the end of which time' she was condemned for a breach of the slave treaty, as having had slave-cargo on board during the voyage, and as not being entitled to the protection of any flag or nation, sailing as she was under nondescript colours, being actually British property, and exercising the rights of a registered ship.

As with the condemnation of the Pachetto my services on the coast of Africa ceased, I shall conclude my narrative, trusting that it may not be uninteresting, and that it will afford you all a few hours' amusement in the evenings; and if I have the happiness of joining you in a few months, it will call to mind places and scenes, and enable me to relate numerous anecdotes of people but little visited and less understood by Englishmen, who annihilate the slave-dealers and civilize Africa by their own comfortable firesides, little thinking of the hardships and privations their countrymen are undergoing to carry out their impossible theories.

CHAPTER IX.

WHEN writing the above I was still suffering
from the effects of fever, and was kept a month
in the hospital undergoing an operation. When
convalescent I joined H.M.S. Thunderbolt as
First Lieutenant, being strongly advised by
the medical men not to return to the coast.
Our first trip was to Natal with the 45th
Regiment; and I had a famous opportunity
of testing the safety and utility of the paddle-

box boats in a heavy surf, through which we managed to land 300 troops in one day, and embark the same number the next, without a single accident. Soon after we started, however, one of those frightful accidents occurred, which, from their very suddenness, startle one and make a deep impression. One of our best forecastle men, of the name of Voller, whilst securing the anchor slipped and fell overboard, and must have been instantly dashed to atoms by the wheel. We of course stopped immediately and sent away the cutter, which returned after a fruitless search.

In September of the same year we were ordered to Mauritius, with stores and ammunition for the Conway, after the affair at Samatave; and I had the happiness of meeting many old friends who had taken me by the hand sixteen years before, when there as a mid; but as, during the fortnight we remained, our time was fully occupied in coaling, I could see very little of them, and left with great regret. Having a fair wind, we did not steam between land and land; and the barometer indicating a gale when we were off St. Frances Bay, we worked in and made all snug, and rode out a heavy monsoon. Whilst here, we sent a boat to a barque which was standing in, and found her to be the English barque Kyle, laden with sugar and very leaky, and her men very much fagged by constant work at the pumps. I assisted her to gain the anchorage, and, at the request of her master, Captain Broke ordered a survey on her, the result of which was a recommendation to tow her to Simon's Bay.

During our passage we had considerable experience in towing a large ship in a seaway. In the first place we tried large hawsers and messenger, but everything in the shape of rope snapped like packthread as this huge ship buried her bows in the water; so we got her bower cable through our stern hawse-hole; and she towed famously for a few hours; but, from a little unsteadiness in her steerage, she gave a yaw which snapped a link; and we then, after a great deal of care and trouble, succeeded in getting the end of our bower chain to her, and, with fifty fathoms between us, towed her at the rate of eight knots without the least jerk, the bight but seldom rising out of the water.

It was not without considerable difficulty that we managed to keep clear of the vessel whilst she was heaving our chain on board, for the least movement of the engines more than requisite would have snapped the hawser. The moment they stopped the two ships were being drawn together; and I had just turned in, well fagged, when I felt the ship tremble violently, and heard a crashing noise, which appeared to be occasioned by all the bolts being drawn out of the deck. Without waiting to dress I rushed on deck, the sentry telling me as I passed him, that the Kyle had run into us, "carried away the stern and rudder," and was tearing us to pieces. The moment I put my foot on deck I saw it all: we had been shortening sail, and the fore-sheet had got foul of the wheel. The order was given to "stop her," and of course the bight of the chain brought the two ships together, and the crash we heard was the doubling up of the stern boat. Fortunately I was just in time to prevent something worse; for the moment she touched us the order was given to go on, and the engines had been already set in motion, whilst this immense, deeply-laden merchantman was broadside on to our stern. Another revolution would have brought the whole momentum of upwards of a thousand tons on the cable, and either torn her bows out, snapped the chain, or ripped up our decks. However, we soon got all right again, and towed her without farther mishap into Simon's Bay, and received £1,200 salvage.

In February, 1846, we took on board troops to endeavour to effect a landing at the Kowie River. On the way we touched at Algoa Bay and took in a pilot, a Mr. Salmon, who had commanded vessels on that coast, and was considered a most enterprising and experienced hand; and as the weather was exceedingly fine, we felt very sanguine as to the success of our expedition, on which not a little depended, as it would have shewn the Caffres that we could throw a body of men into the country bordering on Caffraria whenever we chose. We found, however, a heavy swell all along the coast, and I was sent, with the pilot and Mr. Bodie, a master lent from the Winchester, in a paddle-box boat to reconnoitre; and we found a complete wall of surf all along the beach. To have attempted a landing, even without troops in the boat, would have been courting certain destruction. Independent of a sweeping current setting through intricate channels formed by rocks just awash, which would endanger the safety of loaded and not easily managed boats, there is an almost constant swell, which I have frequently observed for years on this inhospitable shore, exposed to all the fury of the Southern Ocean, with its prevailing south-easterly winds. I should imagine that there are but few days out of the 365 in which a boat could be beached with safety. Now and then, however, small vessels are enabled to run into the river, and there they stick sometimes.

The barometer indicating bad weather, we returned to Algoa Bay, where we landed the troops, and then started once more for Simon's Bay, and shortly after our return the President arrived with the flag of Rear-Admiral Dacres, and relieved the Winchester, which sailed for England on March 1st, bearing with her our best wishes, and many whose friendship and society we had highly valued and enjoyed.

No one who has not actually been from home
for a lapse of years can conceive the feelings
with which we look at ship after ship gradually sinking below the horizon on her home-
ward-bound voyage, and think of the joyful
hearts they contain.

About the latter end of March, affairs began
to look very threatening on the frontier, and
nothing was heard of but fire and destruction
by the Caffres, who were rushing in thousands
on this poor devoted colony. Accordingly,
we were sent to Table Bay, where we embarked a detachment of the 27th Regiment,
and 500 stand of arms for Algoa Bay, on the
27th, and on the evening of the 30th we were
so close to Cape Recife, that we could hear the
breakers plainly; but a strong breeze springing up from the westward, we were obliged to
lay-to under storm-sails all night, and in the
morning we had a specimen of the uncertainty
of the currents on this coast. Generally
speaking, they set to the westward at least
thirty miles in twenty-four hours; but on this
occasion we were the same distance to the
eastward, and found ourselves close to the

Bird Islands, instead of between Cape St. Frances and Recife; so we had to shorten all sail, down masts and yards, and steam up against a strong head wind.

On our return to Simon's Bay, on April 3rd, we found that the President had sailed for Algoa Bay with the Governor, Sir Peregrine Maitland, and, with the exception of towing the Mariner transport to Cape Hanglip, on her way to Port Elizabeth, we had nothing to do until the 11th of May, when we embarked eighty marines, one hundred soldiers, and sixty-five burghers, with a large quantity of arms and ammunition for Algoa Bay. On our passage back, we chased and came up with a Dutch barque about dusk, and were much amused at the commotion we caused on board; for they were evidently labouring under the impression that we did not see the ship, and were about to run her down. Lights were flying about fore and aft, and the bell was being rung furiously; whilst a man sang out, "Keep fadder off!" "Keep fadder off!" I was sent to board her, and found her to be a vessel from Batavia with coffee, &c.

On May 25th, we gave a parting dinner to
our much esteemed Captain Broke, who had
been promoted, and was to sail on the following day in the Mariner; and as nothing but
good feeling and respect towards him had
existed throughout the ship from the date of
her commission, we could not sufficiently express our regret at parting ; and as the greatest
mark of respect we could show him, we pulled
him on board the transport in the gig in our
uniforms, whilst the men gave him three hearty
cheers. Scarcely was he out of sight, when
our new commander, Lieut. Belgrave, received
orders to prepare for sea which, after a heavy
day's work taking in and securing a three
decker's moorings, was anything but agreeable,
particularly as the man-hole doors were off,
and the boilers half scaled. However, we set
to work with a will, and were ready for a start
in five hours.

At midnight, we steamed out of the Bay, taking
one hundred seamen, and twelve marines, from
the President, to garrison Cape Town, where
some disturbances were anticipated. In raising the Burgher force for the frontier, many of

M

the men were paid substitutes, and consisted
of the very dregs of the people; and without
some kind of restraint hanging over them,
would have soon become unmanageable. As
it was, our men kept the town quiet, and
parties of seamen, under the warrant officers,
relieved each other on board the ships taken
up to convey the new levies to Algoa Bay,
and quashed many an outbreak at its very
commencement.

After remaining three weeks in Table Bay,
we received the thanks of the Colonial Government, and left our friends at Cape Town fully
satisfied that British seamen, when under strict
and proper discipline, can act on shore as well
as afloat, and prove themselves anything but
the reckless beings they are generally considered.

On our arrival at Simon's Bay, we found
there the French frigate Armide, and met her
officers at the Admiral's, who gave them a large
dinner and ball, and on the following day
some urgent despatch called the Admiral to
Cape Town, and prevented him from dining
on board the Frenchman. Mysterious reports

began to float about, that we were to go *some-where* immediately, and we were ordered to take in an extra quantity of coal, bread, and spirits ; and I was sent for and questioned about the Mozambique, Quillimane, &c., which eventually proved to be our destination.

At this time, the Kaffirs appeared to have it all their own way on the frontier ; and an article in the "Cape Town Mail," headed, "Loss of Forty-one Waggons," set every one on the *qui vive*, and as all the particulars may not have reached England, I shall endeavour to give some idea of the harassing warfare.

It appears that the waggon-train started shortly after sunrise, under the full expectation of being attacked by the Kaffirs, in charge of Mr. Dixon, who, with a party of burghers, had volunteered his services ; and with Mr. Lucas and thirteen of his troop, took the lead, the infantry being placed in the centre, and the remainder of Lucas's troop bringing up the rear.

On reaching the Blue River they were joined by sixty men of the 91st Regiment, who did not however alter the order of advance.   The

waggons were now at a point where the road
became much broken, hilly, bushy, and tortu-
ous, and here the Kaffirs had posted themselves
to dispute their further progress; and just as
the advanced guard had reached the summit
of the first ridge, a heavy fire was opened on
them from the thick bush and rocks by the
roadside, which killed two horses and a Fingoe.
Beyond this elevated bushy mound, where the
enemy had so strongly posted themselves, was
a small patch of open ground, and the moment
the first volley was fired, the burghers, under
the command of Mr. Dixon, plunged into the
bush, and gained this position. Dismounting
from their horses, the troopers endeavoured to
push their way through the bush with the
waggon, but were met at the same spot with a
most deadly fire which killed five oxen. As
they fell they were cut away from the yokes,
in the hope that the rest would struggle through
the pass, which was only effected by Messrs.
Dixon and Lucas putting their shoulders to
the wheel, whilst the soldiers goaded the oxen
with their bayonets; and in the open space
above mentioned, the burghers took up a good
position.

The second waggon had to pass through the
some ordeal, and as it approached, the Kaffirs
poured in the same destructive fire, which was
steadily and vigorously returned by the 91st,
for about ten minutes ; when a large body of
savages was seen moving down the main road,
with the apparent intention of cutting off the
communication between the burghers and the
rest of the waggons.   They were obliged,
therefore, to fall back on the second one;
losing two civilians, and several horses of their
gallant little body.   By this time the retreat
had become general, and the result of this
disastrous affair was the loss of four men killed
and two wounded, eighteen horses killed or
lost, and forty-one waggons with all their
oxen and stores.   The only consolation is,
that the ammunition-waggons had been left
behind.

The above will give you some idea of the
kind of people we have to deal with when you
hear of war with the savages. Savage indeed
are they, but day by day getting more expert
in the use of fire-arms, and so observant of
our least movements, that I have heard officers

describe their throwing out skirmishers as being
quite equal to our own manœuvres. They are
funny fellows too, hailing our soldiers, and
telling them what they are about to do, throwing defiance in their teeth, and making as
many grimaces and gestures as monkeys. Their
cunning makes them fully aware of the huma-
nity of the English character, which prevents
us from killing an unarmed man; so when they
find themselves taken unawares, they throw
their arms into the bush, pretend to be friendly
Kaffirs, and in all probability fire on our
troops when they get to a convenient distance.

On Wednesday, June 24th, having filled the
after stoke-hole, and stowed ninety bags on
deck, we started, with 380 tons of coals on
board, for the Mozambique Channel, to collect
the squadron and send them to Mauritius to
join the Admiral, who, it was expected, would
proceed with them to Madagascar to endeavour
to open the trade and bring the Ovas to an
account for all their misdeeds. At 4 P.M.,
the wind being fair, we took off the floats,
and averaged six knots until the morning of

the 26th under sail alone; but the wind falling very light, we got under steam, and had scarcely made a fresh start, when a vessel inshore was observed to fire a gun, and we stood towards her. She proved to be the Mary Anne from Madras, with a detachment of the 57th Regiment on board, under the command of Major Shadforth, who, with several of the officers, came on board, and played a very good stick at the ale, porter, bread and butter, one party relieving the other, and making up for ten weeks' short allowance. We gave them the disagreeable intelligence that in all probability they would go to the frontier instead of England, and supplied them with flour, bread, and malt. In the boat that came for the second party of officers was one solitary individual, who no doubt anticipated from the report of his more fortunate brothers in arms, a similar "blow out;" but there is many a slip between the cup and the lip, and our time and steam being precious, he got nothing but expressions of regret that he had not come before, as we were off immediately. Thus faded his visions of soft tack in the smoke, which in about half an hour was all that could be seen of its whereabout.

On the 28th we fell in with the Sappho on her return from Mauritius, and whilst our Commander was on board, her First Lieutenant and Master came to shake us by the hand, as they had orders for old England. We just had time to drink their healths in champagne, when away we started on our respective cruises. A break of this kind, though lasting but a few minutes, varies the monotony of a long voyage, cheers one up, and gives a point for the memory to dwell on when looking back on the past. It tends also to create a good feeling amongst the men, who found many a yarn on such simple events.

Economising our steam as much as possible by working expansively, and taking advantage of every fair wind to unship the floats, we found on July 3rd that the current had drifted us so far to leeward that we were obliged to put on a third boiler to enable us to reach Delagoa Bay before dark. On approaching the land to the southward of Cape Colatto, it makes like a number of small islands; gra-

dually sand hills and sandy patches make their
appearance until near Cape Colatto, when the
country begins to look thickly wooded, and
the north extreme of the island of Inyach is
not unlike Point Natal on a small scale. The
bay is very large, and has a most uninviting
appearance, being studded with hidden rocks
and shoals; and now and then a white-crested
breaker, in what appeared before a clear passage, was quite sufficient warning to keep off;
and as we could see that no ships were at the
anchorage, we shaped our course for Inhamban.
Delagoa Bay is the south extreme of the Portuguese possessions on the east coast of Africa.
They have a small garrison and a Governor.
The slave trade has increased there very much
of late, and a ship sails from there yearly
laden with ivory for the Bombay market.

On the 5th July we were off Inhamban,
and as soon as it was broad daylight observed
what we took to be a vessel under all sail
standing out of the river; and as there are
very few honest traders in this part of the
world we were kept on the *qui vive* for about
an hour, when it was discovered to be a mark

on the land, so we stood along the coast for Luabo, made it on the 7th, ran all day in seven fathoms' water, and in the evening reached the anchorage off Quillimane, where, as usual, the rolling was awful and fully bore out my previous descriptions. Not a soul, I believe, got a wink of sleep that night. In the morning I was ordered to get the pinnace out, and endeavoured to lay out a kedge to spring the ship's head to the swell; but a strong current prevented me; and by watching the roll and letting her go by the run when clear of the gunwale we managed it without any damage, and, after considerable difficulty, succeeded in rigging and preparing her for a trip up to the town, where we had to leave despatches for the Cleopatra.

About half-past nine a party consisting of the Commander, Campbell, Mr. Hamilton, the Purser, Dr. Hastings, a youngster, and myself, started with a fine fair wind and (for Quillimane) a moderate swell, which led me to anticipate but little difficulty in crossing the bar; but, as it happened, we were placed in a most perilous position, for the rollers were setting in much heavier than I imagined, and whilst *running* on the top of a white-crested breaker, the tiller snapped short off in my hand and the boat broached to. Fortunately we were going at such an awful rate that the sails were becalmed and the main-boom did not jib, and by great exertion I was enabled to slue the rudder with my fingers in the tiller-hole before the next sea overtook us, which would most assuredly have swamped the boat had we not received it end on.

My feelings on this occasion were rather curious. In the first place, I had the greatest confidence in the stability of the pinnace, a fine boat twenty-eight feet long with plenty of beam; but, like many of our men-of-war's boats, some inches too low for a surf boat, for I have found from experience on these bars that, when the whole body has to be supported on a breaking wave, the foam is apt to boil over the gunwale, which was the cause of my being filled and capsized in the Cleopatra's gig on the same spot. The remembrance of that awful day is always most vividly present whenever I cross a bar even in fine weather, and has such an effect on my nerves, that although my presence of mind is probably increased by it, and enables me to act on the instant, I find myself after the danger is past trembling like a leaf. On the present occasion no one seemed to be aware of the great danger we were in but myself; but one and all agreed that I had not without reason designated the bar of Quillimane as dangerous and treacherous.

The contrast, however, after getting over it, is pleasant in the extreme, and on this day more particularly so, as it was quite new to all but myself, and very few of the party had ever seen anything approaching to the scene that opened out on them. Instead of rolling and tossing about, it was as smooth as a mill-pond. Hippopotami, pelicans, and numberless birds afforded capital marks for the sportsman; the negroes scattered along the shore fishing, or sailing lazily under the branch of a tree, formed picturesque groups quite novel to the European eye; and, although the freshness of feeling wears off by use, it was no small satisfaction to be able to point out the different objects of interest to my companions as we all but touched the mangrove bushes on our way up the river.

Soon after noon we landed, and first proceeded to the house of my old friend Senhor Azvedo, who was taking his siesta, but soon made his appearance looking very ill with the fever; but still delighted to see us. From him we learnt that Lieutenant Gibson and my brother had been there but a week before from the Cleopatra, on board which ship there had been a great deal of sickness, to which my much lamented friend Alexander had fallen a victim—the second of four of us who left England together and met an untimely end in the execution of their duty. May they meet a happier and a better world! The Helena had also suffered, having forty on the sick list at one time, and her commander, Sir Cornwallis Rickets, had been living on shore for some time at the Governor-General's house.

The information I managed to pick up was most interesting to me, as it corroborated most of what I have before related in the former pages, making something like a finished story of my narrative; and I think my best plan will be to copy the notes I made at the time almost verbatim. The Cleopatra, they said, had "*played the Devil*" at Angonha, taking the Lucy Penniman, an American barque, and burning a brig called the Kentucky, which, strange enough, was the same vessel that I saw at Quillimane under American colours, in company with the Anna. This latter craft, it will be remembered, I took to the Cape after we had captured her off Luabo fully equipped. The Kentucky was also one of the brigs that escaped from Inhamban with a cargo of slaves, when Paulo Roderique managed to get three clear off with 1,500.

The fate of this man was a just one, and a warning to those who spend their lives in amassing ill-gotten wealth. Not contented with his agency of ten dollars for every slave he shipped, he endeavoured to cheat the owners by desiring the captain of one of the vessels to sell fifty blacks which belonged to them, on his own account at Rio. This shipper, however, let the cat out of the bag, and Paulo Roderique lost, not only his expected money for the fifty slaves, but the whole of the agency as well, and was living in a state of indigence at Rio.

Martonhas, the last of the slave-agents here for the Company at Rio, had been obliged to leave Quillimane, having become known to the English, and officially reported to the Governor-General, which would have led to his imprisonment—one of the many instances wherein our information caused the removal of the principal supporters of the slave-trade on this coast, and which did more towards suppressing it than all the captures we made. In about half an hour after our arrival, the Commander and myself paid our respects to the Governor, who received us in bed, to which he was confined by fever, liver, headache, and a complication of chronic complaints acting upon an old and worn-out frame. Of his own accord he touched on the slave trade, which he decried as the most abominable traffic on the face of the earth, regretting that there were not some means *por castijar (with set teeth)* the villains engaged in it. He then named several rivers which the slavers had frequented since we had driven them from Quillimane; but his information was of too general a character to be of any service, and we heard afterwards that he had been superseded and ordered to Mozambique, to answer before the Judge and Governor-General, for conniving at the slave-trade. Poor old man! I trust he will be able to clear himself, for I am satisfied that he was sincere in his professions on his first arrival; but the temptation is almost too great for any man who gets 300 dollars a year paid in dungaree; and who by shutting his eyes for a day or two, may at the end of that time open them and find 15,000 on his table.

After dining at Azvedo's, I went round with Dr. Hastings to visit several sick, amongst others a man who had been wounded the night before. He had been dining with two friends, and before parting they had quarreled; and after he had been in bed a short time a knock was heard at his door, on which he demanded the reason of his being disturbed at that hour of the night? The answer induced him to open the door, when he received the contents of a musket in his right arm, the ball passing behind the shoulder-blade and wounding him in the lungs. Altogether he presented a fearful appearance, and with the miserable attendance he would have, there was but little chance of his recovery.

The slave trade seems at a very low ebb at Quillimane, and the people are beginning to seek for other employment for their slaves, cultivating a great quantity of corn and rice for exportation to Mozambique and Lisbon; and Isidore the late collector of customs, who has been so deeply engaged in the slave trade, has purchased a vessel, which he intends to load with ivory, rice, bees'-wax, and wood, all the produce of Quillimane. He consulted me on the subject of manning his vessel, stating that he found considerable difficulty in procuring a crew, and asked me if I thought it safe for him to liberate a number of his blacks, procure the proper papers for their manumission, enter them on the muster-roll, and clothe them in the European fashion. I told him candidly, after consulting with Mr. Hamilton, that I thought it would be at the least a dangerous experiment, as he would probably find much

difficulty in persuading the officers of every
cruiser that all was right, in which case he
might be subjected to much inconvenience by
detention, and probably have his vessel condemned, if any of the liberated slaves thought
proper to declare that he had been forced on
board against his will.

Many a poor fellow, however, might in my
opinion gain his freedom in this way if the
thing was rightly understood, but there have
been so many instances known of the men
thus emancipated being sold again at Rio after
the voyage, that it is difficult to know what
advice to give as long as the profit of a slave
is about 1,000 per cent.; and I fear much, that
poor blackey suffers as much from the mistaken
zeal of his would-be friends, as he does from
the wretches who consign him to slavery.

I made diligent inquiries about the slave
trade carried on at Angonha, and am led to
believe that it has only of late become a place
for the exportation of slaves for the Brazils,
and that the Lucy Penniman, Kentucky, and
two others which escaped, are the only vessels
which have attempted to take in cargoes there.

The Majojos have, however, for many years carried on a brisk trade in human flesh, by means of Arab dows, with Zanzibar, Johanna, and the Red Sea; but of late, the Sappho, Mutine, and Helena, have taken and destroyed several of these vessels, and put a temporary check on it. But there are so many rivers and inlets on this coast which a man-of-war cannot approach, that we might as well try to alter the currents in the Mozambique channel as stop the slave trade with sailing vessels.

By many it is supposed that the slaves are driven to this river from Quillimane: this is, however, quite a mistake, as the tribes inhabiting the country about Quizungo are independent and warlike, cutting off all communication between the two places; and vast numbers of slaves, with large quantities of gum-copal, and ivory, come from the interior down this beautiful river, which affords every facility for legitimate trade.

In September, 1846, 1,400 free blacks arrived at Quillimane, each carrying an arroba or thirty-two pounds of ivory. They described the place they came from as being nearer

Angola on the west coast than to Quillimane, and they had been fifteen moons travelling, having frequently to fight their way, and living by the chase.   They sold their ivory for coarse blue dungaree, at a ridiculously cheap rate, and returned to their country highly satisfied with their (to them) great riches, and in a few years more a like visitation may be expected. What a famous channel through which to introduce civilization into Africa, and show the savages how much better it would be to engage in this kind of traffic than destroy each other by slavery; but the white man's love of gain is stronger than his power of doing good.

CHAPTER X.

I HAVE on a former occasion mentioned that
the Landines, a tribe of Kaffirs from the neighbourhood of Delagoa Bay, who had been
driven back by the disaffected Boers of Natal,
had overrun the interior of Africa, and they
have now established themselves in the neighbourhood of the Portuguese Prazos, levying
contributions of bales of cloth and other merchandize, in the name of Denjan or that
worthy's son; allowing those only who pay
them tribute to purchase ivory, &c., from the
neighbouring tribes. Oddly enough, whilst

this story was being related to me by Azvedo
one of his own elephant hunters came in,
having done nothing, for fear of these in-
vaders.

A Pole, named Lukomskï, who keeps a
store at Cape Town, has been allowed by the
Governor-General of Mozambique to enter the
different ports on the coast with a large assort-
ment of English goods, for which he is to get
ivory, rice, bees'-wax and other produce of the
country, thus opening an extensive commerce
between these fertile regions and the Cape.
He intends also to combine it with Mauritius
in the following manner: Starting from the
Cape, he will call at all the intermediate ports
between Delagoa Bay and Mozambique; from
this place he will freight a Portuguese vessel
to Johanna and Comoro for bullocks, transship
them, go with them to Mauritius and then
return to the different ports for the ivory, &c.
for his goods left with an agent at each place.
The plan seems to be a feasible one in theory,
but I fear the fever, agents, and detention from
that eternal Portuguese word "Amanka,"
would eat up all profits.

The American brigantine Porpoise, which I boarded in October, 1844, with the crews of two vessels on board that had been turned over to the Brazilians for the slave trade, had been seized on her arrival at Rio by the American Commodore, on suspicion of having been engaged in that traffic, in consequence of which a row had taken place between him and the Brazilian Government, who denied his right to seize a vessel, even under the colours of his own nation, in their waters. She was eventually, however, sent to America to be tried, and I think that I have now pretty well accounted for all the men and vessels, of a doubtful character in the preceding part of this narrative—but now, without doubt, the rogues and slaves we always considered them.

On the 9th we were all engaged to dine with Senhor Morgado, whom I have often mentioned before. At two o'clock, being anxious to make a start for the Point at four, about three we sat down to a most sumptuous entertainment: the first course consisted of twenty-one dishes, and the second of as many more of sweets, preserves, and fruit; and our

host was so hearty in his hospitality and in
giving complimentary toasts, that we did not
get into the boat until half-past five. We were
followed to the beach by our kind entertainers,
who loaded us with all kinds of refreshments.
Azvedo had picked up wonderfully, merely
from the little change of society, and I do not
wonder at their being glad to see even the
English, who are constantly cutting up their
trade; for a more miserable state of existence
than theirs cannot be conceived. Half their
day is spent in sleep, the other half in gos-
sipping and smoking; whilst cut off from all
communication with the rest of the world, they
are dying by inches of a slow fever, which
brings with it a complication of chronic dis-
orders, and very few return to their native
country with the wealth they have amassed.

We gave them three cheers at parting, and
worked about six miles down the river, when
I took the boat too close in-shore, and she
grounded in soft mud; so, after vain endea-
vours to get her off, we had to make the best
of it for a few hours amongst myriads of musquitoes. A rising tide, however, and a light

land-breeze, enabled us to get down to the
bar by daylight. The bar was perfectly
smooth, and we arrived on board at eight
o'clock, much pleased on the whole with our
variegated trip.

We immediately weighed for Mozambique,
and in the afternoon fell in with H.M.F.M.'s
brig Don Juan de Castro, with a Major
Campos on board, the successor to Madeira
at Quillimane as Governor; but we could
learn nothing new of the Cleopatra or Helena
from the officer who boarded us. A rather
amusing incident occurred with him: whilst
in the cabin he wished to write down the
name, &c., of the steamer, for which purpose
Barnes, the clerk, who happened to be present,
lent him a handsome gold pencil-case, which,
after being used, was left on the table. The
Commander, coming in just afterwards, when
I had taken the Portuguese to the gun-room,
and seeing this smart affair, fancied that he
had forgotten it, and said to me, " This would
be rather a serious loss to him," and walked
into the gun-room, presenting it with a very
polite bow. The other very coolly pocketed

it, and it was not until after we had parted company that it was found to belong to poor Barnes.

On the 11th we fell in with a brig under Portuguese colours, and on nearing her I recognized my old friend Dr. Peters, and went on board the Delfana, belonging to and commanded by Trou, the Frenchman, who had the Gentil Liberador when I first came on the station. The Doctor and I were mutually delighted at meeting, and had as long a chat as the time would allow. He was on his way to Inhamban and Delagoa Bay, to prosecute his researches for objects of Natural History, a large collection of which he had already sent to Berlin,—at the expense though, I am afraid, of his constitution, for he looked almost bloodless, and his ears were as transparent as a bit of parchment.

We did not arrive at Mozambique until the 13th, having a current of three miles an hour against us all the way from the Primeiro Islands. The Government pilot took charge of us off the entrance, which, though well known and not difficult, is rather narrow, and

the tides set directly on the shoals. On anchoring, I was sent on shore to wait on his
Excellency the Governor-General on the part
of the Commander, and with the purser made
arrangements with Mr. Nobré for a supply of
wood and water, for I found that we could
not get the latter as heretofore from the
Government tanks at the Fort, in consequence
of their running short the year before, when
the Governor refused to allow the Portuguese
men-of-war to have any, after having given it
to the English. This caused much discontent;
and all ships are now obliged to pay the large
sum of a dollar per pipe. There is, however,
a bay a little to the northward, where our
men-of-war can water themselves. In the
course of the forenoon, the Commander came
on shore, and I accompanied him to the
palace, where we learnt the following particulars about the Cleopatra.

In consequence of the written permission,
which the Governor had given Captain Wyvill,
to enter all the rivers and secondary ports of
the Portuguese possessions on the east coast of
Africa, four boats were sent up the River

Angonha in June, under the command of Lieutenant Gibson, who had young Jago with him in the barge. Lieutenant Hornby had the second gig, Lieutenant Denman the Imaun (a private boat), and Mr. Bagley the cutter. On entering the river they perceived a brig which, on the approach of this formidable force, was set fire to and deserted by her crew. Hornby, however, managed to board and measure her, and found that she was fully equipped for the slave trade, with her coppers mounted on deck ;—and this was the Kentucky before mentioned.

In another branch of the river a barque was discovered, and on being boarded, the mate and several of the crew came forward and asked for protection against the captain, who they declared had brought them there against their will to carry on the slave trade, and was about, they were afraid, to make away with them, and replace them by Brazilians who had been smuggled on board after the ship had left Rio. All this the captain denied; and expressing a wish to be landed, the second gig was given to him. However, on her approaching the shore, the demonstrations appeared so hostile that she laid on her oars until a canoe came off for him, and he appointed an hour for returning; but as the four boats approached the rendezvous, a brisk fire was opened on them from the bush within thirty yards, which was returned with grape, canister, and musketry, until the ammunition was nearly expended; when seeing no signs of the captain, they returned to the barque with four men wounded, and took her out to the Cleopatra. I was much pleased to hear that my two young friends, Jago and Bagley, had behaved with the greatest coolness under fire.

This barque was the Lucy Penniman, which on a former occasion brought cargo to purchase 5,000 slaves at Quillimane; and in the present instance had been loaded with goods for the purpose of obtaining cargoes for three vessels, two of which actually escaped from this said River Angonha. She was placed in charge of Mr. Chase, the American Consul at the Cape, who communicated with his Government, and she was eventually given up to her owners, and has, I dare say, long ere this found her way to the same profitable waters, where the chances of escape are so many. In fact, with American colours she runs no risk, if the captain and crew are true to each other.

The Cleopatra had also driven another vessel on shore at Delagoa Bay, which was taken possession of by the Portuguese soldiers, and afterwards taken by Lieutenant Hornby and my brother John to Mozambique, where she remains until it is decided by the Home Governments whose prize she legally is. Most probably she will be sold, and start afresh as soon as the Cleopatra goes off the station.

The Governor-General had sent an ambassador to the chief of the Majojas at Angonha, threatening to send a force and punish him severely if he persisted in carrying on the slave trade. For this purpose he will probably ask for the assistance of the English squadron should he get an unfavourable answer. In the meantime, the chief of his own accord wrote to the Governor, complaining of being attacked, and declaring that he was not aware " that there was any harm in making slaves ;"

that they made them at Quillimane, and why should *he* not make them?

I inquired why the Governor of Quillimane, Abreu de Madeira, had been superseded, and found that it was for countenancing Martinhas, the slave agent, and afterwards allowing him to escape after he had been ordered to imprison him; and the old General declared he would shoot one of them as an example, if they persisted in conniving at the slave trade. He has already recalled two from Ibo; and Major Campos, whom he has now sent to Quillimane, is an old soldier, has seven musket balls in his body, is much trusted by Government, and appears averse to the slave trade; but he must be a wonderful fellow if he resist the chink of dollars, with the certainty of being laughed at afterwards for his scruples.

On the 14th, finding that the wood and water did not come off fast enough for our English ideas of doing work, I was sent on shore to endeavour to purchase any old wrecks or wood on the beach, and I succeeded in getting a large dow, apparently about 100 tons, built of very hard wood, and strongly fastened with iron.

The breaking her up seemed at first rather an arduous task, and everybody I asked told me I should take two days and a half—the Portuguese said a week; however, we set to work with a will about 11 A.M., and by 2 P.M., the beams being all sawn through, we got two ropes on her; got all our hands, and about 300 blacks on them, and roused her broadside out. By 5 P.M., she was demolished, and two-thirds of her on board the ship.

The scene on the beach during this operation was one of the most exciting and amusing I have ever witnessed, and will long be remembered at Mozambique as an astonishing proof of English strength and perseverance. Our large powerful stokers, with arms like legs, making enormous sledge hammers fly round their heads like paddle-wheels, rending large masses of timber at every blow, appeared like giants to the poor half-starved looking devils who are obliged to have a slave to open their eyes of a morning. Hundreds of men, women, and children were employed knocking out the nails with stones, and for every nail they had to carry a load down to the boat, for which purpose I kept a quarter-master constantly loading them, so that the dow appeared to be actually walking into the sea. Poor darkie entered into the spirit of the thing, and when large masses came down with a crash, they yelled with delight. Poor degraded beings, how much might their condition be improved! but here they are ground down to the lowest state of human degradation, and it is frightful to contemplate beings so little raised above the brute creation in a place which has been in the possession of Christians (so called) for hundreds of years.

The Commander, Mr. Hamilton, and I dined with the Governor-General, and met Captain de Valle, commanding the brig Tejo, and senior officer of Her Most Faithful Majesty's naval forces in the Mozambique. He has been several years in the English service, and speaks our language perfectly. He seems in earnest about putting down the slave trade, and has commenced operations by sending out the Villa Flor with sealed orders,—a capital plan, as it will bother the slave agents, who have been in the habit of conveying information to

the rivers about to be visited; for although
there is no slavery at Mozambique itself, all
the merchants are more or less interested in
its being carried on elsewhere.

The master of an American barque told me
that two or three captains, who had sold their
vessels at Rio, and afterwards brought them to
the coast of Africa under American colours,
had been subjected to a fine of 10,000 dollars,
and five years' imprisonment, which looks as
if the United States' Government was in earnest
in putting down the slave trade.   He had been
recently at Majunga (Madagascar), where he
had not been permitted to trade, or even to
sell his powder, the Queen—or rather her ministers—being determined to have nothing to do
with foreigners.   He says that the people
themselves are most anxious to trade, and
much dissatisfied with the existing state of
affairs, caused principally by two men who
have an English education, and have managed
to get the whole government into their hands.
He states also that the heir to the throne, a lad
about fourteen years of age, and son of the late
Radama, is beginning to look about him, and

to wish to put an end to the present troubles;
so I shall not be surprised at hearing that the
ministers have lost their heads, or been obliged
to take poison, an alternative generally allowed
to those obnoxious to the stronger party.

· On the 15th, at five in the morning, I took
a party on shore, and brought off the remainder of the dow, with numerous pieces of
the main keels of large vessels, which had
proved too heavy for the Mozambiquers to
remove. So I bargained for them for ten
dollars, and cleared the beach in a very short
time. I also tried to induce them to exert
themselves for once, and give us an extra turn
of water; but a shrug of the shoulders and
their favourite "Amanhâa" (to-morrow) was
all I could get out of them; so we had to
send our own men with breakers. During the
day we were visited by the whole of the free
population of the place. First came five boat
loads of Banyans in their white flowing robes
and turbans of cloth of gold, and each one
thought it incumbent on him to shake me by
the hand as he came on deck. Their costume
is picturesque enough, but I prefer it in the

back-ground; so I soon got a large pile of
fire-wood between us, by sending them with
the corporal to see the ship. The boats of
the Tejo then brought on board all the ladies
of Mozambique, a motley-looking group of
yellow, snuff-and-butter, and dingy-brown
beings, with new rigs made for the occasion.
To describe them it would require one to have
lived in the days of our great-grandmothers,
when short waists and up-and-down figures
were in vogue; and they looked so uncomfortable in their thick dresses, warm enough
almost for an English winter, and shoes large
enough for men, that we had enough to do to
keep our countenances and do the polite.
However, they were highly delighted with
their entertainment, and showed by their
parting signs how grand they thought it all.

We got clear of the pilot by five, and
unshipping the floats stood to the northward
with a fine fair wind for two days, when being
off Cape Delgado, the extreme of the territory claimed by the Portuguese, we looked
into the bay; but seeing nothing, put our
head off the coast of Africa,—that land of

slavery, debased human nature, disease, bribery, and corruption; the grave of many a fine noble fellow who has been sacrificed to the impossible theories of orators who have never been out of England, and look more to the immediate effect of their speeches on the people than the ultimate result.

On the 18th, the current having set us considerably to the north, we got the steam up and commenced on our wood, 38,000 small billets of which we had got on board, besides the dow and wreck of all kinds, filling the space of about 100 tons of coals. It cost us 172 dollars. The commander, master, and myself, remained on deck most of the night, and passed the island of Comoro about midnight. It is very high, and we had seen the outline of it for some hours. The next day was a Sunday, and a lovely morning it was; the fine high land affording a most pleasing contrast to the uninteresting, low, flat, miasmatic-looking coast of Africa; and having no sails set the men had the day to themselves. About 9 p.m., we fired a gun, and soon observed lights in the direction of

the town of Johanna, the peak of which is
5,900 feet high: the anchorage is but a few
hundred yards from the beach in about ten
fathoms water; but a quarter of a mile outside this, there is no bottom with 100 fathoms;
and if one has not been there before, the ship
appears to be running bang on shore. Just
before we struck soundings, the masters of
three American whalers came alongside,
having seen our lights, and very civilly put off
to offer assistance. They "guessed" we must
have found it pretty considerably *rugged* outside, as it had been blowing strong for a week
previous; but they calculated that we should
now have a quiet spell; and certainly a quiet
night was most acceptable after the awful
rolling we had experienced for some days.

The next day, at five in the morning, we
got the boats loaded with casks, and commenced watering in a beautifully clear stream
close ahead of the ship, running direct from
the mountains; with our small engine, we
filled as fast we could hoist it on board. The
island is one of the most striking and picturesque that can well be imagined, being a con-

stant succession of high and peaked mountains
and deep valleys, the latter clothed with verdure, whilst the former are crowned with cocoa-
nut trees, with their gracefully curving leaves
relieving the outlines of the hills, which are
green to the very summits.[*]

After breakfast, the commander waited on
His Majesty Sultan Selim, who with all his
suite came on board. Amongst them I recognized several old acquaintances, but I have
so often described them before that I shall
avoid repetition. The Sultan was most
anxious to see the machinery at work, and at
30 minutes past 11 we weighed and stopped
opposite the capital, Mountsanouda, where His
Majesty disembarked. It is a regular Arab
town, consisting of piles of black-looking
houses with narrow alleys instead of streets;
dirty in the extreme, although the inhabitants
are constantly in the habit of visiting all our
possessions in India, Mauritius, and the Cape,
and are extremely fond of dress, rigging themselves out in all kinds of gay colours.

On July 22nd, we were off Cape Amber,
the north end of Madagascar; but a strong

head-wind and lee current obliged us to put
out the fires, to save our fuel and put her
under sail; and for the next ten days we had
a most anxious time of it, taking advantage of
every lull or slant of wind to make our coal
last us, for the south-east trade in these seas
approaches a gale, and knocks up a most awful
sea, which brings up the engines all standing.
However, by constant attention and perseverance, making sail when we could, and getting
every thing down when under steam, we
managed to reach Port Louis on the 2nd of
August, having been under steam twenty-five
days in July alone; and the wood we took in
being only equal to twenty-one tons of coal, we
may consider that the old Thunderbolt did her
work well, having had upwards of 4,000 miles
to run, without taking into account all the
deep bays we ran into along the coast, and
760 miles of adverse current. Besides this,
we had to work up against a strong and
squally trade right in our teeth for 700 miles.

The admiral had arrived in the President a
week before us, and we were all rather disappointed at the expedition to Madagascar being

given up. On the whole, though, I feel sure
that it was the wisest course, as it would take
a much more considerable force than we could
have sent there to have made a lasting impression. For three weeks we had a constant
succession of gaiety and amusements, and
although the prevailing complaint seemed to
be a scarcity of provisions and money, I never
yet saw a place in which so constant a round
of feasting, dancing, and late hours, is kept up.
There is a very good French opera, and the
races which took place whilst we were there
caused considerable excitement and a large
assemblage of people.

But by far the most interesting and beautifully got up affair was a fancy bazaar given by
Lady Gomm: the proceeds are intended to be
applied to the completing the tomb of an old
French Governor on the Champ de Mars.
The large quadrangle in front of Government
House was arrayed as an immense tent, covered in and tastefully decorated with foreign
ensigns, suits of armour, &c.: it was crowded
with well-dressed people, and produced £800.

I went to two or three of the sugar estates,

and, as it was during the harvest, had a famous opportunity of viewing the whole process of sugar-making. Their great drawback is want of labour which, when they can get it, is very indifferent; at least one-third of the miserable race that arrive from India being constantly in hospital, and even for these there is such a competition that their wages are enormous. Worse than all this, however, are the restrictions under which the planters suffer; for the apprentices being only bound for one year, their services finish just as they begin to know something and to be useful. Machinery will, I dare say, in time supersede a considerable portion of the manual labour; but the planting, cleaning, and manuring the ground, and gathering in the crops, will always require a great number of hands, and almost all the estates are so involved that it takes more than half the profit to pay the annual interest of their debt to the merchants.

We had a famous run of twelve days to the Cape, arriving in Simon's Bay on September 3rd, and found a good opportunity of sending our letters home by the Sappho and Resistance. In the latter, our new Commander, Alexander Boyle, had arrived and took charge, and on the 20th we started for Algoa Bay with Colonel Slade and five subalterns for the frontier. We were three days on the passage, having a south-easter to steam against, and our engines were not powerful enough to force so large a vessel against a head sea, her speed being soon reduced to six and a half knots.

At Algoa Bay we took on board forty trusses of hay from the Commissariat, and started the same afternoon for an *indent* in the land, (so called) Waterloo Bay, and fortunately arrived on the first day on which there had been any communication with the shore for a month. So we succeeded in landing everything and in embarking 160 of the Burgher force, who would otherwise have had to walk some hundreds of miles; and a poor, miserable, half-starved, half-clad, set of wretches they were, several suffering from typhus fever or ague brought on by exposure and bad diet.

My old messmate, Charles Forsyth, who had the temporary berth of Harbour Master there, and has been mentioned in the Governor's despatches as having done good service on more than one occasion when troops had to cross the Fish River, came off to us and accompanied the commander on shore, where the Governor, Sir Peregrine Maitland, was encamped about three miles from the beach, having been obliged to fall back on the provisions which had been landed here at an immense risk and expense. The troops had suffered great privations, not having been able to make any impression on their subtle enemy, who, if he continue the same kind of harassing warfare, will not be conquered for years. The Governor was roughing it out in a small tent with a common deal table and stool, and every body seemed astonished at a man of his great age being able to go through so much anxiety and fatigue and still appear as well as ever.

The next day very heavy rollers set in and rendered it impossible to communicate with the shore, excepting by signal, and there being no prospect of a change for the better we started for Algoa Bay to await the arrival of the Lieutenant-Governor, Colonel Hare, who had resigned, and was succeeded by Colonel Somerset. This day was one of the most disagreeable and anxious I have ever experienced. There was a strong wind with heavy showers in the squalls, and a thick mist quite hid the land at times, although we were running close along it. The poor Burghers, who were in a most ragged condition and too numerous to stow below, looked the picture of misery and discomfort, sheltering themselves as well as they could under sheepskins and karosses. Towards the evening, as we approached the Bird Islands, we had to keep a constant and anxious look-out, and the ripple caused by the current and a heavy sea had frequently the appearance of breakers; and at last, when we did make these islands they were not more than a mile right a-head of us. However, we steamed up to the anchorage by half-past nine, and the following day being fine soon got the ship dry and comfortable, and set the poor Burghers on their legs again.

On September 29th, Colonel and Mrs. Hare and a small suite embarked, and the next day

we landed twenty-eight of the Burgher force in
Mossel Bay, where there is a small fishing village miserably supplied with fresh water, which
is quite open to the south-east. The fishermen
here refused to land their returned comrades
without being paid, which we all thought was
rather a cool reception after all their fighting.
On the morning of the morrow, after vainly
attempting to steam round the Agulhas against
a strong wind and heavy sea, we bore up,
passing close to that dreaded point on which
so many valuable lives and ships have been
lost. On the beach were the remains of the
Gentoo, an American barque, and a brig which
had been sent to take her cargo in after she
was wrecked. We anchored in Struys Bay,
just round the point, until the following morning, and anchored in Simon's Bay the same
evening, just before the Inflexible from England,
which brought us late news and letters.

The latter end of October we took in two
sets of heavy moorings for Waterloo Bay, and
went round to Table Bay, where we embarked
700 bags of bread and grain, and fifteen
waggons. We then took the barque Sir

Edward Ryan in tow, full of mules; and, following the plan we had before found so successful with the Kyle, took in her bower chain through our stern hawse-hole, and towed her without a jerk as far as Cape St. Frances, when a strong south-easter obliged us to cast her off, for we made but little headway, and she was rolling most fearfully without any sail. On the following day we arrived in Algoa Bay in time to ride out a heavy gale, and see five vessels driven on shore from their anchors and totally wrecked; and it was not for some days that the sea went down sufficiently to enable us to land the waggons; after which, taking a large surf-boat in tow, we started for Waterloo Bay, and arriving early in the morning, were fortunate enough to find a smooth beach, and to get rid of a great portion of our bread and grain, besides laying down both mooring-anchors.

The next morning, after getting rid of the remainder of the grain, we started to the northward to look for the Buffalo River, having on board as pilot an old shipmaster named Findlay, who had landed provisions there for the troops during the last Kaffir war, and on making the land he recognized several head-lands near the anchorage; but as soon as the sun was high enough to get an observation, we found that we were between twenty and thirty miles from the river called the Buffalo in Owen's chart. However, the old man was quite right in his recollections, and we found ourselves off a pretty-looking winding stream, just round Point Hood, and anchored in six fathoms, about three-quarters of a mile from the shore.

The country about presented the appear-ance of the most beautiful park-land, dotted with clumps of trees; and immense herds of cattle were quietly grazing on the brows and sides of the hillocks; and as we stood along shore we could see every here and there a few stray Kaffirs taking stealthy peeps at us, and almost immediately disappearing. Gradually they be-gan to assemble in knots of twenty and thirty above where we were anchored, several with soldiers' coats, some with muskets; but the major part with spears only; and we could distinctly hear them hailing us, whilst they played all kinds of monkey-tricks with their arms. One of the paddle-box boats and the cutters were armed, and the commander and master sounded the entrance of the river, and found that the depth gradually decreased to three fathoms.

A cable's length from the shore, and at dead low water, there were five feet on the bar, with from eight to twelve feet just inside close to the left bank, where the landing is perfectly easy; and from the first we were convinced that this would be one of the principal advanced posts when our operations extended into Kaffirland. From the whole appearance of the country, and its being the only river we have seen on this coast where communication can be kept up without the aid of surf-boats, I should say it will one day become a valuable settlement. The anchorage, unlike that at Waterloo Bay, is quite free from rocks, and fish is so plentiful that, in about an hour, enough was caught to supply the whole ship's company.

Thick and rainy weather came on the following day, and, when it cleared up, we found that the current had drifted us considerably

o

to the southward of Algoa Bay, where we touched to send the result of our survey to the Governor, and fully expected to have many a trip to, and perhaps be the first to establish, a post in so desirable a spot—little thinking, after all our narrow escapes on this danger-ous coast, and our great good fortune and success in landing more provisions and stores in one day than many merchant-vessels had managed in months, that I should have to relate the loss of the Thunderbolt.

Before this, however, we had a great deal of cruising about between the different bays along the coast, carrying troops, arms, and stores of all descriptions for the force on the frontier, our boilers and engines never keeping us back one hour when our services were re-quired, although they had been in constant wear for four years. Our last trip but one was in January, when we were sent to Algoa Bay for Sir Peregrine Maitland, who had been recalled; and after rounding Cape Recife in a heavy westerly gale, we were, although under the lee of the Point, enveloped in spray like a thick mist; and it was with the greatest difficulty we could make out the headlands to steer by through this narrow passage. However, the next morning it moderated, and we steamed back to Simon's Bay in forty-five hours.

CHAPTER XI.

I NOW come to the most painful part of
my narrative,—to that calamity which de-
troyed our prospects, ruined our hopes, and
lowered us from the height of joyful anticipation, to the greatest depth of misery and ruin.
Expecting our relief daily, we were, after
being highly complimented on our order and
efficiency, ordered to Algoa Bay, to embark
the 90th Regiment; and on the 3rd of February, after a most splendid run, we were just
rounding Cape Recife, and standing towards
the anchorage, when, at 5 h. 40 m. P.M., we struck

heavily twice on a sunken rock, going at the time upwards of nine knots. The master was on the paddle-box, and the commander had not left it more than a minute, and was on the quarter-deck giving me some directions relative to the sails before getting into harbour. We had a leadsman in each chains, and a man at the masthead, and every usual and necessary precaution had been taken to prevent accident.

As officer of the watch I had been particularly attentive to the conn under the direction of the commander and master, and did not consider, from where I was standing, that we were rounding the breakers closer than usual; but from its being nearly high water, spring tides, with an unusually smooth sea, they could not have extended nearly as far off shore as on previous occasions; for as far as I could judge we were at least half a mile from them.

The shock was severe and the vessel reeled, though not so much as to lead us to suppose that the injury was so very serious. We were soon, however, painfully undeceived by the

first engineer's report that the water was
rushing into the engine-room with the greatest
fury. Every preparation was immediately
made for the worst, first by taking the injection water from the bilge; but unfortunately
the starboard injection cork having been
damaged when we struck the port, one only
would act. With one watch the pumps were
manned and all the buckets in the ship kept
at work, whilst the other watch turned over
the paddle-box boats, got the cutters ready
for lowering, triced up the pinnace's purchase,
and supplied each boat with fresh water, the
officers and men from the commander down-
wards working as coolly as if at exercise.

All this time we were making the best of
our way to the anchorage, the water gaining
rapidly on us and our speed fast diminishing;
and the water in the engine-room was getting
so hot that the men could scarcely stand in it
to feed the fires. The ensign was hoisted
union down, and guns were fired at intervals,
which, about 6h. 30m. P.M., brought the port-
captain, Lieutenant Jameson, alongside, and the
commander immediately determined to run

the ship on shore as the only means of preventing her from going down in deep water.
Indeed, in ten minutes more the fires would
have been put out, as those in the wing were
already extinguished; so at 6h. 41m. the poor
old Thunderbolt was run on the beach not far
from the spot where we had seen so many
others not long before brought to an untimely
end.

The pinnace was hoisted out and the stream
anchor got into her and laid down astern; the
best bower anchor and cable were then warped
out by it and hove well taut, whilst a kedge
was sent above high water mark and a seven-
inch hawser laid out to it from the ship.   At
midnight the water was level with the steerage
deck and still rising; but thinking we might
take a few hours' rest, a watch was set and
the hands piped down.   By one o'clock, almost all hands had got soundly asleep after
their great fatigue, but by two the water had
reached the cabin deck, and the gunner, who
had been left in charge of the watch, was obliged to call us up.

An indescribable scene immediately ensued,

each person getting his clothes, &c., on deck, where they were heaped together in one confused mass, most of them being well saturated before they could be rescued; and by four the tables in the cabin and gun-room were afloat, and we could save nothing more. At daylight the surf-boats landed the ship-company's hammocks and bags, and afterwards the officers' traps, which were placed in the commissariat yard and covered temporarily with sails. At high water we found seventeen feet water under the stern, and at low water, twelve, the tide ebbing and flowing inside the ship. During the day, Lieutenant Campbell superintended rigging tents on the beach, whilst on board we got the derrick rigged for getting out the guns; unbent the sails, and landed all the stores we could get at.

At 5 P.M. we left the ship for the night, it not being deemed safe to remain on board, and took up our abode in the tents; and a pitiful and heartrending sight indeed was it, to look upon our beautiful craft which it had been our pride to devote our whole time to, and feel that probably all our labour had been in vain; and many an eye was dim and voice broken that in the hour of ·danger had remained unaltered and steady. But we did not give ourselves much time to indulge· in vain and useless regrets, for on the 5th every thing that ingenuity could suggest and zeal carry out was commenced in good earnest.

Mr. Langley, the first engineer, with his brother officers and all the artificers, undertook the construction of large and powerful pumps on shore, whilst on board we prepared to take the guns into deep water, by lashing two surf-boats together with three spars and round about lashings well frapped together ; and buoying them with lengths of 9-inch ·hawser, to which were attached large water-breakers, and these were again buoyed with lengths of spar in the event of their sinking. ·The breechings answered for slings to ·hoist ·them out, and the sea-gripes for slinging them between and outside the boats; and in ·this manner, after a great deal of anxiety and considerable difficulty from a heavy ground swell, we managed to take out at one time the two 10-inch and·two 8-inch guns and drop them without cutting a rope yarn in five and a half fathoms' water.

The ship to-day appeared to be resting on her centre, and to be much strained: one of the deck planks was broken, and the framework of the engine was cracked. She had also settled down six inches more by the stern. We continued to get out the stores, diving to clear the sail bins, and starting overboard as many coals as possible from the starboard bunkers, as she had a list to starboard which was her wounded side; and we did not land until seven, the men having worked like horses.

On the 6th we still had fine weather and hoped for the best, placing and fitting five large pumps. Their dimensions were nine and a half inches square in the clear, with a nominal stroke of nine inches, but on trying them we found that they would not work up to more than seven inches, making forty-two strokes in a minute, and throwing an immense body of water. The only wood that could be obtained in the place to make these pumps was 3-inch fir plank, one foot wide, which we were obliged to saw into one and a half inch, as, had we kept it the whole thickness, the bore would have been so much reduced that they would have thrown a very inconsiderable body of water. A party was employed thrumming a sail, and in the afternoon sixty men of the 90th Regiment came off to assist in trying the pumps, which we found made no impression on the water; so we fitted three more, and at 11h. 30m. P.M., commenced pumping and baling again, and passing the coals from the starboard side to the port.

We persevered until 3 A.M. of the 7th, when we found the water gaining on us, and discontinued, landing the troops as soon as possible; and shortly after five, the rapid approach of a strong south-easter, with a heavy swell, obliged us to land and take all the boats on shore. Although Sunday, the engineers, artificers, and four of the 90th, continued hard at work constructing pumps, but the strong wind threw in a nasty sea which made a complete breach over the poor devoted vessel. However, on the 8th it moderated, and we managed to get on board, and found much less serious damage done than we had anticipated, as she did not appear to have strained much, although all the stern bulwarks were washed away and the deadlights stove in. By means of a hauling line, we sent on shore all our spars and rope not likely to be wanted, and got a great quantity of coals out of the starboard bunkers, whilst the stokers were taking off the paddle boards; and during the afternoon we were much pleased at finding that we could turn the wheels with tackles, which proved that the engines would still work; and in the evening we landed, and found several more pumps ready.

On the 9th we got off in our own boats and fitted seven additional pumps, the artificers still making spare gear for them on shore. In the afternoon, eighty men of the 90th Regiment came on board; but, as we had expected two hundred, we were obliged to accept the offer of Captain Hogg, who commanded a large body of Hottentot Burghers and brought off one hundred of them. At 3 P.M., our preparations being complete, we commenced pumping with twelve pumps constructed on shore, and our own two, whilst parties baled at each hatchway.   At first we gained rapidly on the leak, but by midnight the pumps began to break down; and though the engineers and carpenters were indefatigable in replacing and repairing the boxes and stopping the leaks, we soon saw it was a hopeless case, although we put a good face on it, and cheered up the men, who were getting dreadfully fagged and disheartened.

On the morning of the 10th we still persevered; but found, as the water got lower, the pumps would not keep tight, notwithstanding all our woulding, double nailing, and stopping every crack with white lead; still they threw a good stream of water, and we managed to gain slowly on the leak, whilst by clearing the starboard coal boxes, we gave her a list to port, and the water did not appear to rush in so rapidly, which made us fancy that the thrummed sail and swabs had been sucked in.

At daylight we got fifty seamen from the merchant-vessels; but our old enemy the south-easter setting in strong, we were obliged to land the soldiers and burghers before the surf rose too high, and at 10 A.M. left the ship once more, with all the boats; and in the afternoon the sea once more swept her decks. The artificers still continued to make more pumps, and had the Eurydice and President made even an average passage from the Cape, and arrived at this time, I feel confident we should have saved her, as the bulkheads were still perfect, and no dirt had been washed into the bridge, which will be seen hereafter was the ultimate cause of our being obliged to abandon her.

On the 11th it fell calm, and on going on board we found that the ship took the ground more, and fore and aft, and to lie much easier; the creaking of the beams above the boilers had ceased, and the planks that had been broken had sprung back into their places. On trying the pumps we gained four and a half inches in eleven minutes, but knew that it would be useless to make any attempt without many more, which the artificers worked away at with a right good will, whilst the rest of the ship's company aired and stowed away the stores, cleaned the arms, &c. By this time our great exertions and frequent disappointments had become quite the theme of conversation on shore; and although for the most part they looked upon it as a hopeless task, we met with every assistance, and knowing what perseverance will sometimes accomplish, we were determined to prove that English seamen are not easily beaten.

On the 12th we put strong parties on the pumps, woulding and strengthening them in every possible way, and in the afternoon, by means of one of our own paddle-box boats, on a surf line, we managed to get off six more pumps, and at six I took all hands on board, ready to commence pumping in the morning. Wrapping ourselves up in sails on deck, we endeavoured to buoy up our spirits with the anticipation of success on the morrow.

On the 13th, at daylight, two hundred of the 90th Regiment came on board, and at eight we commenced pumping with eighteen pumps, made on shore, our own two, and parties baling wherever there was room, and during the first hour we gained two feet seven and a half inches; but, as the pressure on the pumps increased, every little leak admitted air, and during the sixth hour we only gained six inches. At 1h. 30m. P.M. the ship was alive fore and aft, and remained so for three hours, bumping heavily until the tide fell; and at 6 P.M. we were enabled to light the fires in the starboard foremost boiler, and at nine the steam was up, and we got about twenty revolutions at intervals; but the steam from the one boiler was soon worked out, and the ship having a list to port, we could never get the water low enough to light the port fires. Hour after hour did we watch with intense anxiety a mark we had in the engine-room, but there stuck the water, sometimes half an inch above and then the same below. The night was pitch dark, the men dreadfully fagged, and a very small proportion of the pumps delivering their water. However, we worked away at the coals, and about eleven the captain of the hold told me that he heard the water rushing in just before the engine-room bulkhead, in the wing; so I immediately crept in over the tanks and saw a strong stream, which I reported to the commander, who for hours indefatigably superintended removing the tanks and clearing away over the leak, which extended much farther aft; for, after forcing in numbers of bread-bags, wedges, and shoring out the broken timbers, the water increased on us as much as ever; and we used the utmost exertion to get a few of the broken-down pumps into repair.

On the 14th we still continued pumping and baling, keeping the men at the pumps with great difficulty, for they appeared quite worn out and disheartened at seeing that their labour was in vain; and, as a last resource, Mr. Langley disconnected the starboard engine, trusting that we should have steam enough with one boiler to work the other; but before it could be completed, the water got up to the fires, and extinguished them as well as all our hopes (for that trial at least), and at 3 A.M. we discontinued work, after nineteen hours' incessant labour.

At daylight, the approach of a south-easter obliged us to leave the ship, and, notwith-standing our failure, we should still have suc-ceeded in the end, had not the elements been against us; for we had found eighteen feet of the leak, cleared away the coals from it, and found the machinery uninjured.

On the 15th and 16th, matters began to look very serious, and the heavy sea that had set in was breaking furiously over the ship, which had shifted her position, presenting her quarter to the sea.   The beach for miles was strewn with wreck, and the men were divided into parties, to save all we could in the shape of ladders, gratings, and paddle-boards.   We could see from the shore that the port paddle-box was washed away, the pumps thrown out of their places, and almost every thing that we had based our hopes on, destroyed.   However, we set extra parties to work on more pumps, and were far from despairing of ulti-mate success.

On the 17th, we managed to get on board, and a scene of destruction presented itself, which we shall none of us easily forget.   In the first place, she had settled so deep in the sand that the water was three feet deeper inside than out, and at low water the port gunwale was level with the water's edge;

the bulwarks, and everything connected with the port paddle-box had been washed away; every bulkhead, fore and aft, was floating about below, leaving a clear run for the sea fore and aft, which blew out the fore-scuttle during the gale as high as the fore-top. The after-part of the upper deck had all started, and several of the planks had been blown up and floated away; the casing of the funnel had disappeared, and all the pumps were much wounded, and many of them destroyed. At the first glance almost all hopes of saving the ship had fled. However, 'the commander consulted with the master, Mr. Langley, and myself, and we all agreed that our best plan would be to land and repair the pumps, prepare and sling a number of casks to assist in righting her, get as much weight out as possible, and wait the arrival of the men-of-war.

Fortunately some planks which we had bent over the stern had withstood the sea, and the hull of the ship was not apparently strained; so we again set to work, took out the sheet-anchor and let it go by the guns, landed the pumps, agreed with a cooper for a hundred casks, and in the excitement of preparation, forgot all our disappointments and misfortunes.

On the 18th we commenced early at the pumps, and a party on board was employed clearing the wreck, and saving what stores had been left by the gale; but at high water the deck was covered, and we were obliged to land, as the sea swept her fore and aft. In the afternoon we commenced slinging the water-casks, and the Eurydice made her appearance, which cheered us up considerably.

On the 19th the President hove in sight, and having the assistance of the artificers and men of the Eurydice, our work became lighter and less tiresome; for one and all of her officers devoted themselves entirely to our service, and were just as anxious as ourselves. In the night the commander with myself and all hands, assisted by a party from the Eurydice, got several casks into the port paddle-wheel and turned it with tackles; but there was a nasty swell on, and the great number of holes in the deck make it a very difficult and dangerous task, so that the water rose and drove us out of the ship before we had got half as many as we had hoped in a position to buoy her up.

At 2h. 30m. A.M. of the 20th we landed, returning at nine to make our preparations for a last attempt at pumping her out at low water, battening down the hatchways, stopping the holes in the deck with paddle board and mess tables, and frapping and battening a thrummed sail over the stern, strong parties from both ships assisting us.   By noon our preparations were complete, and we had rigged twenty-three pumps made on shore, four from Simon's Bay, and our own two.   The after-part of the port gunwale was two feet under water, and the wash of the swell came up to the combings of the hatchways; every seam in the deck leaked, and the sail kept the water but very partially from running freely into the stern windows.   However, we were cheered up by finding that the immense body of water we threw out of her soon made a sensible im-pression, and in a very short time she began to right, assisted as she was by a great number of casks, which we continued to rouse under the

sponson. Our force was divided into two parties
of three hundred men each, relieving each other
at intervals of from four to six hours, and
working in three spells of twelve minutes
each.

During the afternoon we procured several
iron pumps from the shore to supply the places
of the broken-down ones; for notwithstanding
all our care and precaution, the pumps made
on shore were not strong enough. Still we increased rapidly on the leak, and at 7h. 30m. P.M.
it was high water and she bumped heavily for
two hours, but apparently without straining.
At midnight we gained very slowly indeed, and
during the darkness of the night, it was impossible to repair the damaged pumps. However
we hoped to make a fresh start at daylight,
and the officers of both ships never flagged for
one instant, keeping the time and arranging
the spells with the greatest regularity, whilst
the men toiled away without a murmur. Our
anxiety was, however, increased by the approach of our dreaded enemy, a southerly
wind with its accompanying heavy swell.

During the middle watch of the 21st we
just held way with the leak, and at five I
took one watch of our own men on shore to
breakfast, for they had not been relieved from
the first; and after snatching two hours' rest
we again returned, taking with us two more
iron pumps which we had raised out of wells,
their owners willingly lending them. The
commander then went on shore with the other
watch, and we began to gain on the leak again,
our extra pumps doing good service, and daylight enabling the artificers to repair the damaged ones. At 11 A.M. the master of the
Eurydice (Rodgers) succeeded in getting our
main-topsail under the bottom, after which we
reduced the water so rapidly that by noon the
fires in the starboard foremost boiler were
lighted. In the course of the afternoon the
Eurydice's lower studding-sail was got round
over the main-topsail, and a large party kept
continually working away at the coals and
laying bare the leak. By 4 the steam was up,
and at 4h. 50m. we started the port-engine,
which would only work at intervals with the

one boiler; and the port foremost one being damaged it was some time before we could light the fires in the after one. By six, however, the engine worked continuously and reduced the water rapidly, the plates in the engine-room beginning to show themselves.

I now considered that the ship was saved, and so did the commander, as she was afloat fore and aft bumping only occasionally, and had moved a considerable distance out of the bed she had made for herself. I was accordingly ordered to lash the purchase. I sent to the President for anchors and hawsers, and merely waited for the opinions of the captains and practical men to haul her into deep water. Captain Stanley, Captain Anson, Commander Boyle, and the carpenters of the three ships, now examined the leak most carefully, as far as it could be seen, and it was found to be so extensive that the carpenters declared that, if even what we had discovered was the extent of the injury, they *could not* make her seaworthy for a voyage to Simon's Bay. It was also considered unsafe to haul her into deep

water unless the engineer could guarantee to
keep her free with the engine, as the pumps
had done their work, having been merely constructed to reduce the water below the fires;
and on consulting Mr. Langley, it was found
that the engine was not taking the injection
water as it ought, a circumstance supposed to
arise from some tow having been sucked into
the jet pipe inside the condenser. To have
remedied this the steam must have been shut
off for at least two hours, and even then the
want of tools and materials would have made
it a very doubtful job.

This, however, might all have been over-
come, had not the rapid approach of a south-
easter rendered it unsafe for the men to
remain on board all night, so that after pumping her out all but dry from the beams of the
upper deck, and floating her under the most
trying disadvantages, we were obliged to
abandon her and allow her to sink again. At
seven the engine was stopped, and the men
returned to their ships with great difficulty, as
the sea was fast getting up, so much so, in-

deed, that several broke into our boat as we landed. During the afternoon the beach had been lined with all the inhabitants of Port Elizabeth, who, seeing the ship afloat and the engine at work, thought, like ourselves, that we had saved her; and their disappointment in the morning at finding that we had given her up was second only to our own.

Thus ended all our hopes, which had enabled us to work incessantly for three weeks against the furious attacks of the elements with almost unheard-of success, inasmuch as we actually pumped our ship out dry, and floated her; and had not a small pipe been choked, by an accident against which every precaution had been taken, until the sea swept every obstacle before, fore and aft, H.M.S.S. Thunderbolt would have still been on the navy list, an evidence of what ingenuity and perseverance can accomplish; for I have no hesitation in saying that no man-of-war ever had a better, steadier, or a more well-ordered crew, or a commander who devoted himself more to his ship and the service. Indeed, his decisive and cool conduct throughout, and total disregard of self, won golden opinions from all who witnessed them; and Captain Stanley told me, whilst we were all standing over the leak in the coal bunker, that our exertions had been almost incredible, and not to be conceived excepting by an eye witness, and that, whatever was the result, we should at least have the satisfaction of feeling that we had done our duties faithfully and zealously.

The following is a calculation of the quantity of water thrown by the different pumps:

First 23 square pumps, $9\frac{1}{2}$ inches in the clear with a stroke of 7 inches, and working 40 strokes in a minute, threw in one hour 562 tons.

Four ships' pumps of 6 inches diameter and 7-inch stroke, threw in one hour $38\frac{1}{4}$ tons.

Two Downstones and two Erles, $43\frac{3}{4}$ tons nearly in one hour; making a total of 644 tons an hour.

This average was kept up, by baling and the constant supply of iron and other small pumps from the shore.

I have allowed 277 cubic inches to a gallon,
and 224 gallons to a ton.

During the two following days we were
unable to communicate with the wreck or the
frigates, but we could observe the President
getting in our guns and anchors, which they
found in as good order as when we let them
go. On the 24th we were enabled to get on
board, and parties of artificers were employed
in saving anything of value that could be got
at; and in the evening the President sailed for
Simon's Bay with the head-quarters of the
90th Regiment, taking our sick and the cutters.

On the 25th, we unrigged the lower masts,
got the bowsprit out, and in the afternoon
embarked on board the Eurydice, the soldiers
striking and clearing away the tents; and on
the following day the approach of a south-
easter determined Captain Anson to sail, as at
least three days must elapse before we could
have again communicated with the wreck;
and by the indefatigable exertions of Mr.
Hamilton, our purser, whose activity had been
invaluable to us during our severe trials, the

bills were all settled in a few hours, and with aching hearts we quitted our poor old Thunderbolt at 4 P.M., with her lower masts standing, and two anchors out astern.

Nothing could exceed the kindness and consideration we met with from the officers of the Eurydice, who had from the first made our misfortune their own; and after a beautiful run we arrived at Simon's Bay on March 2nd, with rather different feelings from those we usually experienced when taking in the moorings in our own rakish-looking steamer.

We found the Hazard and Wolverine here on their way from China to England, and learnt that we were to be divided between the two vessels and sail on the 7th, which was rather short notice. Anything, however, was better than being kept in a horrid state of suspense, and the prospect of so soon getting to England, made us forget every inconvenience.

The admiral gave the commander the greatest credit for our exertions; and he, in common with all the inhabitants of the colony, looked upon our disaster as the loss of an old friend.

On Sunday, March 7th we made sail for old England in the Hazard, the Wolverine having started the day before with one-half of our officers and men; and we could not help contrasting our present circumstances with what they might have been in our own beautiful steamer, instead of crowding up the officers of a small ship, who had barely room for their own things. Indeed, at first it seemed next to impossible that one-half of what we had saved could be got below. However, affairs soon began to assume a better aspect, and the kindness of our new messmates made us feel ourselves at home and comparatively comfortable. Fine fair winds took us to St. Helena in nine days and a half, the Hazard and Wolverine anchoring within an hour of each other.

The next day we got news from England by the Pekin, only twenty-three days on her passage, and I met on board her Colonel Mitchell, who was on his return to the Cape

with authority to commence a lighthouse forthwith on Cape Agulhas, and I understood on
Cape Recife also, both of which would save
double their cost yearly in property, and much
more in valuable lives.

THE END.

LONDON:
Printed by Schulze & Co., 13, Poland Street.

CPSIA information can be obtained
at www.ICGtesting.com
Printed in the USA
LVHW051414120120
643319LV00011B/462/P

CPSIA information can be obtained
at www.ICGtesting.com
Printed in the USA
LVHW051414120120
643319LV00011B/462/P

9 781165 275328